To Joel,
& L...,

Good luck with the
gin project.

David T Smith

The Craft
of Gin

Written by

Aaron J. Knoll
& David T. Smith

WHITE MULE PRESS
AMERICAN DISTILLING INSTITUTE

© 2013
All rights reserved.

ISBN 978-0-9836389-6-4
P.O. Box 577
Hayward, CA 94543

whitemulepress.com
distilling.com

Contents

Preface

The Craft of Gin is a short introduction to the world of gin produced by craft distillers in the US, the UK and worldwide. The book takes you through the colorful history of gin, introduces the different varieties of gin and explores craft gin distilling as it is happening today. Explore gin at every step of the production process from the botanicals growing in the field to interviews with some of the distillers who are honing the craft of gin right now. *The Craft of Gin* also covers the canon of "essential gin cocktails," all the way from the Aviation to the Gin & Tonic.

Newcomers to the world of craft gin and enthusiasts will like our sections on tasting notes and gin trivia. Chapter 4 includes tasting notes for over 50 gins from four different continents. This project included a two-day tasting of almost 40 different gins from 30 different states. In Appendix II, you will find some gin questions to help solidify your gin knowledge; these are arranged by chapter and include a few extra nuggets of information as a bonus.

The book has been great fun to research and write and we hope you will enjoy reading it and continue to explore the craft of gin.

Thanks goes to all the distillers who helped us with the tasting and technical specifications of all of the gins featured in the book. A special thanks go to those distillers who were kind enough to contribute their interviews to the book. Thanks also to the countless others who gave help and advice through the writing process.

Seventeenth century Plague Doctor with a beak full of juniper and other botanicals.

Chapter One

On Gin

THE ORIGINS OF JUNIPER FLAVORED SPIRITS

To find the beginnings of gin, we must look far back in time to the intersection of man's discovery that juniper berries had use beyond medicinal purposes and the technology of the still.

Classical cultures, such as the Greeks and Romans, used the humble juniper berry for a wide array of uses: increasing one's athletic vitality, treatment for headaches and toothaches, and even in conjunction with other herbs as a contraceptive. One farsighted Roman philosopher, Pliny the Elder, even foresaw the juniper berry's potential as a food additive and flavoring agent.

While the Greeks and Romans utilized the juniper berry for medicinal purposes, others experimented with the idea of distillation. According to writer and alchemist Zosimos, the alchemist Maria Prophetissa created the tribikos, a device we would recognize today as a three column still, in the first century. Using that knowledge, Jābir ibn Hayyān, an eighth century Persian alchemist, built upon the body of knowledge on distillation and created the alembic still. Jābir is largely credited as being the inventor of the still that laid the groundwork for the modern pot still, though the alchemical craft of distillation had to be refined further over the course of several centuries of work. Though Jābir's device was the most efficient still to date, he was using it more as an alchemical novelty rather than strictly for the distillation of ethanol. Muhammad ibn Zakariya al Razi, Persian physician and pharmacist of the ninth century, saw the potential of distilling for delivering curative agents, rather than the creation of drinkable spirits. It is he who is largely credited as the forefather of alcohol infused with botanicals, and therefore in some indirect way can be seen as the great, great, great, grandfather of modern gin.

Throughout the medieval era, the works of these men and woman spread to Europe. Juniper, already a common apothecary ingredient, was added to distilled spirits during that era. The Dutch were drinking "juniper berry water" recreationally in the sixteenth century; the English were drinking large quantities of distilled spirits to protect them from disease such as the plague. Seventeenth century plague doctors wore distinctive masks with long beaks filled with various herbs and aromatics including juniper to help protect them from the dreaded disease. Coincidentally, juniper is actually an effective flea repellent, so although the Europeans at the time did not understand that fleas were transmitting plague (they thought it was bad odors or miasma, hence the beak full of herbs) those that used juniper were unknowingly warding off the small biting vectors of the plague. For this and many other reasons juniper was on every apothecary shelf, and the berry would soon be all over Europe.

THE BEGINNINGS OF MODERN GIN

The gin we are familiar with today began to take form in what is known today as the Netherlands. The recreational juniper berry water drunk in the sixteenth century came from distilled wine. But why did the base spirit of gin shift from wine to grain? Some writers have theorized that the end of the Medieval Warm Period and the onset of the "Little Ice Age" in the mid-sixteenth century contributed. Parts of Europe which had never been frozen underwent deep freezes for the first time since the last Ice Age. Encroaching glaciers eradicated small villages in the mountains, and the finicky grape plant became more difficult for farmers to grow. This, combined with the volatile political situation around Europe, the Dutch were unable to import enough wine to continue making their juniper berry water with distilled wine. Grain was now in style, out of necessity.

This grain-based juniper-water is known as genever, which still survives to the present day. Bols, one of the earliest distillers of genever in Amsterdam, has continually turned out the spirit since 1664. While genever is rich and malty; the taste is closer to an unaged whiskey rather than a London Dry Gin, thanks to the grain base. For the next step in gin's evolution, we look to perhaps the most familiar place in the world of gin: Great Britain.

William of Orange unknowingly set the stage for gin when he ascended to the British throne in February, 1689. He came from The Hague in the Netherlands, and of course, he drank genever. Historians have noted that the lower-classes and courtiers of the King's court often sought to emulate the practice of the wealthy nobility, and with a gin-drinking King, who could resist? William of Orange not only made gin a popular drink, he made it financially feasible for British-made gin to take root. He declared war on France, and as a casualty, French Brandy was no longer able to be imported. He passed the "Act for the Encourageing [*sic*] the Distilling of Brandy and Spirits from Corn." This act abolished the monopoly previously held by the Company of Distillers, and the floodgates opened. Anyone could distill. Further, it made the duty on corn so cheap that, from a financial perspective, British corn was now the most cost effective base on which to create spirits. Not only was gin popular, but locally sourced gin became the best thing around.

As a result of gin's newfound popularity and ease of fabrication, Britain saw a 400% increase in gin production. The so-called "gin-craze" shortly followed as the streets of London were overflowing with cheap British-made gin. All people in all walks of life at all times drank gin: from business meetings to doctor's visits, men and women alike. Drunkenness became ubiquitous along with warning stories that claimed many of the lower-classes were destroying their lives with "mother's ruin." Historical analysis of the "craze" ranges from claims of hyperbolic exaggeration to serious comparisons to the modern day drug epidemics in the United States. In response to the "craze," Parliament placed high taxes on gin and gin sellers to discourage consumption, with little affect. Later, Parliament tried to ban the production of gin; but suffice to say, prohibition was not well received and resistance emerged. It was in this era of prohibition that the legend of "Old Tom Gin" arose.

In the United States, genever was present in taverns all across the colonies before the revolution, and the taste for genever persisted throughout the nineteenth century. Whilst the Old Tom style (gin that had been sweetened) reigned supreme in Europe, Americans drank gin spirits that more closely resembled whiskey. With the emergence of the London Dry style, gin truly began to take off in the states. While the United States also has a strong gin heritage, the biggest contribution to the lore of gin comes not with the spirit itself, but the in the practice of crafting cocktails.

The British invented the mixed drink. Punch was popular in the mid eighteenth century, and there are reports of tavern owners serving a mixed drink of sweetened gin and some sort of bitters. Cocktails such as the Old Fashioned and the Pink Gin were designed in this tradition, but a lot of what we consider the canon of cocktail-craft came out of American re-imagination of this British tradition. Americans mixed a wide array of spirits with each other, with fruit juices, with wines, with spices and even with vinegar. The British may have invented the mixed drink, but with the Martini, the Manhattan, and the Tom Collins, Americans turned the cocktail into the phenomena it is today.

The prevalence of cocktails aside, the 18th amendment to the United States Constitution which prohibited the production, sale and distribution of alcoholic spirits in the US and its territories, closed thousands of distilleries in the United States. Even though prohibition ended in the 1930s, its impact on peoples' attitudes toward distilleries and the state legislation that governed them persisted. It is only in the last five years that the United States has seen a resurgence in craft distilling, following the popularity of craft brewing. As of 2011, the American Distilling Institute reported that there were over 250 craft distilleries in the United States.

In early 2012, more than eighty distilleries in over thirty states were making gin, with more opening all the time. These new American spirits have pushed the boundaries of what gin was thought to be. Some gins experiment with completely new botanicals, relegating juniper to the background or seeking to complement juniper in new and unique ways.

These novel styles have been given different labels by the press, ranging from "New Western" to "New American," and any number of variations in between. The term "Contemporary" (as opposed to the Classic style gins which largely originated in Great Britain) seems a more apt description for the style characterized by novel experimentation with new botanicals and especially botanicals grown locally where the gin is made. While this style is embodied by many American distillers, "Contemporary" seems more appropriate as these new variations of gin are not exclusively being made by US distilleries, just as Classic style gins are not only made in Great Britain.

Whilst some gins are a stark departure from the Classic British style, some distillers seem keen to bridge the gap between Classic and Contemporary styles of gin. These gins, which are neither strictly classic nor contemporary in character, are sometimes referred to as Trans-Atlantic or Anglo-American Gins. This first term is a nod to actors such as Cary Grant and Katharine Hepburn who had accents that were neither British, nor American but something in between. These accents were quite popular in Hollywood films through the 1960s and were once taught as the American Theater Standard. Though less common today, the legacy of Trans-Atlantic English lives on in gins such as Rehorst Gin, Junipero Gin and TestBed which try to marry the best of contemporary gin practice with the history and legacy of the classic British styles.

Once again, the United States seems to be poised at the front of a reinvention of something that was honed and developed by the British. These are surely exciting times to be a part of the craft distillation movement in the US.

In summary, although gin began in apothecaries and pharmacies, it spread and flourished from the lowlands of Northern Europe to the taverns of North America. It was made into a malty grain spirit by the Dutch, and it became a pawn of British politics as well as the subject of a great number of regulations. Gin was prohibited and then re-permitted in a matter of years, and it has undergone a series of evolutions due to changes in personal tastes.

Gin continues to be an exciting spirit and one to watch in upcoming years. Every year there are more gins on the market than the year before, and although the familiar names are still there, the real cutting edge is happening in the distilleries and minds of those on the frontier.

OLD TOM

Most of the gin being drunk during the early eighteenth century was not quite up to the standards we hold today. A great deal of gin was sweetened to hide the rather harsh byproducts of the distillation process. The grain used was often of poor quality and the end products were sometimes cut with noxious elements like turpentine. So, naturally, to make the end result palatable, they were often sweetened with sugar. This style of sweetened gin is known as "Old Tom."

The legendary origin of the name of this style of cheap, sweet gin dates to the time of a crackdown on illicit distilling in London. It is said that a person could insert a coin into a slot underneath a picture of an Old Tom Cat and a dram of gin would be dispensed. Today's Old Tom Gin is not cut with toxic substances or made from cheap grain (thankfully), but the concept of a sweetened gin has persisted.

As late as nineteenth century this style was still favored by many drinkers, even though distillation techniques had improved enough that sweetening was no longer necessary to cover up the taste of base spirit. Therefore, for much of the 1800s, most of the gin available was sweetened. Men like Charles Tanqueray, Alexander Gordon, and Felix Booth helped to professionalize the distillation industry and made both sweetened and unsweetened gins. The latter being the modern botanical-forward gin, built on a nearly tasteless base spirit. Some of the names that were a part of this movement are names that we still see on gin shelves today.

Around this time, innovations in distilling were plentiful. The column still was patented by Sir Anthony Perrier in 1822 and his invention increased the amount of usable alcohol that was available at the end of the process. Though Perrier's design laid the groundwork, the major breakthrough came from a tax collector by the name of Aeneas Coffey. His patented modifications to the column still design allowed for what would have originally been multiple distillations to occur in a single pass. The end result was a base spirit that we might recognize today: one that is cleaner, lighter, brighter, and which has a higher proof.

Now that the base spirit was clean and clear, gin was ready to undergo another evolution in style, largely driven by a change in the tastes of the public. Victorian tastes preferred a more "healthful" version of the spirits that they had grown accustomed to. "Dry" was chosen as a term to specifically refer to a kind of gin that was unsweetened. This style gained sway among the upper-classes and it was not long before many gin distillers were proudly advertising their "dry" gins, which the gin-loving public bought up. Tastes had changed and the sweetened Old Tom style gradually fell out of favor;

Gordon's, one of the last producers of Old Tom, ceased production of their version in the 1960s.

Old Tom Gin, and the cocktails that call for it, then fell into obscurity until 2007. That year, Hayman's Distillers, a family descended from James Burrough the founder of Beefeater, released an Old Tom Gin, the first available in the UK in over 40 years. Hayman's gin was based on a family recipe from the 1860s. Since then, a plethora of products have followed and today, Old Tom Gin falls broadly into four categories.

SUGAR SWEETENED

The first is sweetened with cane sugar; this is often coupled with the underlying gin being more botanically intense (e.g. Hayman's), but not always. Gordon's Old Tom Gin was actually described as "Gordon's London Dry Gin with Real Cane Sugar." Examples include: Hayman's Old Tom Gin, Goldencock, Both's, Master of Malt's Old Tom Gin and The Dorchester.

BOTANICALLY SWEETENED

In this second style, no sugar is added at all; instead, the sweetness comes from the botanicals, typically licorice. Examples include: Jensen's and Secret Treasures

AMERICAN STYLE OR "OULD TOM"

The most popular style made by craft distillers in the USA. It is sometimes sweetened, but the style is always closer to genever then gin and is also aged in wood to some extent. Examples include: Ransom, Downslope, Sound Spirits, Spring 44 and Corsiar's Major Tom.

IN NAME ONLY

There are some gins that have Old Tom Gin on the label, but this is not in reference to the style of the gin inside the bottle, it is just a name. Examples include: Wray & Nephew's and Boord's.

LONDON DRY

Although various Old Tom (sweetened) Gins are made today, the vast majority of gins are "dry." It is this unsweetened style of gin, that allowed the nuances of the botanicals in a gin to shine through. The flavoring and distinguishing characteristics of a brand of gin were no longer based on sweetness. Distillers began crafting gins based on an array of botanicals to stand out in the crowd. Many of the botanicals that are seen as hallmarks of the London Dry style (juniper, coriander, angelica, and orris root) were first experimented with during the early days of the Dry style.

Presently, the terms "London Gin" and "London Dry Gin" are legally protected by European Union regulation. The regulation is very specific but the rules only apply to gins sold in the EU. London Gin must have juniper as its primary flavor, only use neutral spirits and can have next-to-no (less than 1/10th of a gram per liter) post-distillation sweetening or additional flavors added after distillation. At present only London Gin can be supplemented with the term "dry" in the European market.

However, this is not to say that other gins do not have a dry flavor profile. In fact most gins, Old Tom aside, have a dry character. It is important to distinguish between "London Dry Gin" referring to the production technique and "dry gin" as a descriptive term for the gin's flavor profile. The term is not regulated in the United States; therefore it is not unusual to see the word "Dry" appended to any gin which is not sweetened (and usually has a classic profile as well).

NAVY STRENGTH

Another style of gin that is still readily available today dates back to another walk of life in eighteenth century. While ordinary seamen drank rum, officers drank gin. The spirits supplies were often kept near the gunpowder which posed a potential problem. Therefore, the British Navy only allowed high-proof spirits aboard their ship since their primary function was not drunkenness, but ensuring the verity of their armaments. In response, Plymouth made a Navy Strength gin, at 100 British proof (57% ABV), such that if the gin spilled on the gunpowder, it would still ignite.

Chapter Two

On Making Gin

Gin is a unique class of spirit. The designation "gin" simply refers to a spirit which is at some point flavored with juniper. There are a few methodologies that distillers use to impose the flavor of juniper berries upon spirits and the end results vary in terms of price and flavor.

DISTILLED OR INFUSED

There are two main ways to make gin: it can be distilled directly with the botanicals, or botanicals can be infused directly into a neutral grain spirit. Both methods are known to make high quality gins. First, we will take a look at the methods used by makers of distilled gin.

"Distilled Gin" is the most common type of gin produced by the major distillers. Most craft gins use this methodology because it results in a sophisticated, and delicate spirit popularized by many of the torchbearers of the classic, London Dry style like Tanqueray and Beefeater. Distilled Gin is flavored in one of two ways: the botanicals are placed in a gin head or gin basket during distillation, or the botanicals are macerated, and then added directly into the pot still before being distilled. In both cases it is important to note that the botanicals are added prior to distillation.

Distilled gin has a simple production method. First, a base spirit is distilled, usually from fermented grain to a high proof spirit, often approaching 95% ABV. The resulting spirit is then redistilled with the botanicals held in a device called a "gin head" also known as a gin basket or gin hat. This method of distillation is similar to the Carterhead still. Generally, the gin basket is placed near the top of a distillation column where the alcohol vapors, often around 115°F, pass through becoming "infused" with the flavor of the herbs. The resulting distillate is clear and contains the flavor of the botanicals.

Vacuum distillation, which permits distillation at lower temperatures, is used by some as a point of difference in creating distilled gin. When vacuum distillation is used the botanicals can be placed directly into the spirit and distilled, without the need for a gin basket. Oxley and Greenhook Ginsmiths are among those using low temperature distilling techniques to produce their gins. Some distillers claim that by not over heating the botanicals the flavors are better preserved and it creates a more flavorful, and authentically flavored gin.

Many distillers distill all of their botanicals in a single pass; however, other methodologies exist. For example, some do a distillation of a each botanical individually; this method is used by Sacred Gin of London (UK), Leopolds of Colorado and Moore's of Australia. In this case, each botanical is distilled to create a single flavor distillate; juniper berries for a juniper distillate, coriander seeds for a coriander distillate and so on, these distillates are then blended together to create the final gin. The advantage of this process is that it can ensure a more stable and predictable gin from batch to batch. The downside is of course time. Gin which is distilled flavor by flavor, will take as many distillations as there are botanicals, resulting in a much more time consuming product.

Another method for creating gin stems from the technical specification that any juniper flavored spirit is a gin: gin can be made by simply infusing juniper into a neutral base spirit. Recipes abound on the internet for this kind of DIY home brewed gin which can be made with any vodka. This kind of gin is pejoratively referred to as "Bathtub Gin," however, the name should not lead you to believe that a high quality gin cannot be made with this methodology.

One large advantage of this infusion method is cost. A distiller can purchase a large quantity of neutral spirits and create a gin without ever distilling a single drop. This method is commonly used by some of the inexpensive brands of gin seen in local liquor stores. A second advantage of this method is that it delivers a bolder flavor where more of the subtle nuances of the botanicals can be seen. Some craft distillers use this method to their advantage by highlighting different aspects of juniper that cannot be tasted in the end result of a distilled gin. Bendistillery in Oregon makes their flagship Crater Lake Gin by infusing juniper in a neutral base spirit after distillation. Bathtub gins, more commonly referred to as compound gins, often have a slight tint to them as result of the botanicals being added post distillation. Though often looked down upon by gin purists, Bendistillery has demonstrated that compound gin can produce a high quality spirit.

BASES AND NEUTRAL SPIRITS

Interestingly, gin is in a rather unique situation among spirits. When it comes to its base spirit, gin is an agnostic, in that gin can be made from the fermentation and distillation of almost any agricultural product. The base spirit for most gins is made from a grain such as wheat or corn; however, there are myriad exceptions, from the common place like molasses (most commonly used in rum), to the obscure like honey, apples or even carrots.

EXAMPLES OF GIN DISTILLERS USING NOVEL BASES FOR THEIR GIN

Distillery	Spirit	Base
Flag Hill Distillery	Karner Blue Gin	Apples
Tuthilltown Spirits	Half Moon Orchard Gin	Apples
Warner Edwards Distillery	Warner Edwards Gin	Barley
Finger Lakes Distilling	Seneca Drums Gin	Grapes
G'vine	G'Vine Nouvaison & Floraison	Grapes
Still the One Distillery	Comb9 Gin	Honey
East African Breweries	Uganda Waragi	Millet
Greenalls circa 2012	Tesco Gin	Molasses
Maine Distillery	Cold River Gin	Potatoes
English Spirit Distillery	Dr. J's Gin	Sugar Beet
Knockeen Hills	Heather Dry Gin	Whey
FEW Spirits	FEW Gin	White Whiskey

Since 2010 there has been an explosion in the American micro-distilling scene among distillers using base spirits which have more in common with a white whiskey than your average neutral spirit. These gins have a malty, warm, character that more closely resembled Genever than it does your average London Dry. Examples include: FEW Spirits' FEW Gin out of Evanston, Illinois; New England Distilling's Ingenium Gin out of Portland, Maine; and Smooth Ambler Spirits' Greenbrier Gin out of Maxwelton, West Virginia. GILT Gin made in Scotland creates their gin upon a base of new make Scotch. In short, the above list is by no means exhaustive, but should hopefully illustrate just how wide ranging the options available to a gin distiller are, and show that the creativity that is just now becoming widespread among the American distilling scene is in fact, just the tip of the iceberg.

Chapter Three

On Juniper & other Botanicals

JUNIPER

The juniper plant has been known to man since the dawn of civilization and, in that time, it has been a part of a wide variety of cultures. Many groups have recognized juniper's taste as a desirable one; some cultures used the berry as a flavoring, or as a way to enhance athletic performance. Others used the wood of the plant to make containers, or the bark to make ropes. Monks burnt the branches as part of prayer offerings, while some peoples made tea from the leaves.

Medically, juniper has been used by many different peoples for a wide variety of purposes. In the first century A.D. Dioscorides wrote of juniper's diuretic and antacid properties. In the works of Nicholas Culpepper, the London herbalist and doctor wrote of juniper's utility in treating the bites from venomous animals. Natives of the American Southwest also used juniper, and as recently as the 1918 Spanish Flu, pandemic doctors found it to be effective. Hospitals in the United Kingdom used juniper's aromatic vapors to help prevent the spread of disease. Sadly, juniper's actual medical properties are much fewer than writers might have otherwise indicated. Juniper is an effective appetite stimulant and diuretic. Its vapor qualities might make it soothing on the skin of someone who has been bit by a venomous animal; however, its medical qualities end there.

It is not surprising that may different civilizations experiment and have experimented with the near-ubiquitous bush. There are few places in the world where juniper cannot grow. The entire family of junipers is hardy and, although it has preferences (sun, acidic soils, and some water), it can persist in spite of sub-optimal conditions. In some places, juniper is even used to protect soil banks against erosion, since even drought cannot easily end the hardy shrub. It is one of only a very small number of plants whose range encompasses almost any altitude between 0 and 10,000 feet. Unsurprisingly, there is a lot of diversity within the juniper family. There are almost seventy species, subspecies, variants and hybrids that grow in the wild and in gardens around the world.

Despite its hardiness and ability to grow almost anywhere, juniper made headlines in 2010 across the world when a 2004-5 survey of the British countryside found a troubling decline in their local numbers since the 1970s. Fortunately, scientists were not about to let juniper fade into obscurity in the land best known for so many big names in gin. Plant Life, a wild plant charity from the UK which emphasizes awareness and conservation, has established the Lowland England Juniper Project to formulate a concerted effort to help restore juniper to prominence in the English countryside. Thankfully, juniper is not considered by any conservation agency to be in any danger on a worldwide scale. It can, and will, grow almost anywhere.

Most junipers bear edible berries – although, technically speaking, the "berries" of a juniper bush are actually cones. What makes them a cone, and not a berry, is the fact that fruits evolve from the ovary of a reproducing plant and the juniper "berry" does not. To make life easy for the rest of us, however, the cones of a juniper are colloquially known as berries or fruits.

Juniper berries range from useful and delicious (Juniperus Communis), to edible but rather foul tasting (Juniperus Monosperma), or to outright poisonous (Juniperus Sabina). The most widely-used juniper berry comes from Juniperus Communis, which literally means "the common juniper."

The Common Juniper is indigenous to Northern Asia, Europe, and North America, and can currently be found around the world. It is rather flexible and can grow in nearly any kind of soil, and thrive even in states of neglect, which explains how this scraggly, slow-growing bush has persisted even in ornamental gardens to this day. The bush rarely grows more than ten feet tall, with the branches spread out wide and low, arching up towards the sky. It has a thin, rusty brown colored bark, which is often obscured by leaves and branches. The cones of the juniper are as slow-growing as the rest of the plant, taking 18 months to ripen fully.

The taste of juniper is poignant and bright, refreshing and loud, with a touch of bitterness. This is what gives juniper that distinct peppery mouthfeel, and which contributes to the drying sensation, or that distinctive pal-ate-cleansing aftertaste. Its distinctive flavor and aroma are largely what have made it an important part of so many cuisines. Juniper appears prominently in the Alsatian, Germanic, Mediterranean, and Scandinavian cuisines. In modern day cooking, you are apt to find juniper paired with strong flavored game birds and other wild game. Duck, goose and venison are commonly ac-companied with juniper, but lamb, pork and even salmon also pair well with it. Often juniper is crushed, or used as part of a marinade, rather than eating the cones directly.

One question that has arisen as of late on the flavor of juniper is a ques-tion of location. Much like grapes, cooks and distillers alike have wondered if where a juniper berry is grown (its provenance) can affect the actual taste of the berry. Master of Malt, a bottler out of the United Kingdom, developed a line of juniper-only gins to test this question. In these gins, the only differ-ence between batches is where the berries grew. The line demonstrates that there is an element of terroir involved in the selection of botanicals for gin. For example, the gin made with juniper grown in Veliki Peslav, Bulgaria tast-ed "bright," "floral," and almost close in taste to a contemporary styled gin. Others, such as the batches from Meppel in the Netherlands and Arezzo in Italy tasted "wet and piney" and similar to the taste of a "classic styled gin." So while the bush is hardy and can grow anywhere, distillers of the future will certainly be aware of the way region can alter the character of the fruit in a rather significant fashion.

CORIANDER

Nearly all gins contain coriander, making this arguably among the most important botanicals to understand when considering gin. Two parts of the coriander plant are typically used: the fruit, when dried is referred to as co-riandi, dhani, or most commonly coriander; and the leaf, best known as ci-lantro.

Coriander is native to the Mediterranean Sea region, growing in both Southern Europe and Northern Africa, where it entered into the cooking traditions of the peoples in these regions. Most coriander used in gin today comes from the Mediterranean, Morocco and Russia, although Australian distilleries often prefer to use coriander grown in Southern Australia.

Coriander seed adds citrus and herbal notes, with the Russian-grown seeds having an extra citrusy character. Cilantro adds a sharper, leafy, herbal, and slightly soapy citrus flavor. Cilantro on the other hand is rather uncom-mon in gin, which is notable when considering that coriander is one of the most common botanicals. The rise of the contemporary styles of gin has seen an increase in the prominence of these flavors in gin; one English craft gin uses five different varieties of the plant in their botanical mix.

Both types of coriander are used in cooking and were traditionally used

iris flower and orris root

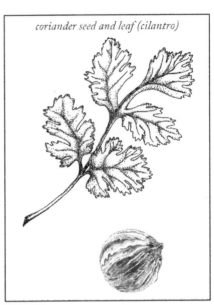

coriander seed and leaf (cilantro)

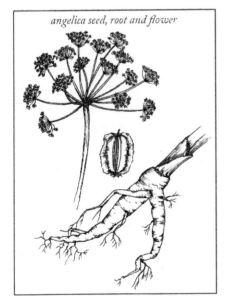

angelica seed, root and flower

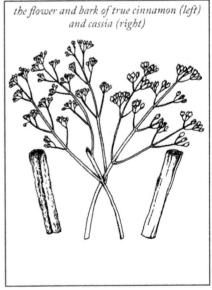

the flower and bark of true cinnamon (left)
and cassia (right)

as an aid to digestion and to treat insomnia. They are also used in the production of other alcoholic beverages, such as Vesperato, beer, Parfait Amour and Bénédictine.

ANGELICA

Angelica is the third most prevalent botanical in gin production and although it is typically the sweet, dried roots of the plant that are used, some gins also make use of angelica seeds.

Although there are over 60 species of angelica, the one used in making gin is *Angelica archangelica*, which is commonly known as Garden Angelica or Wild Celery. It is part of the carrot family and closely related to celery, as well as several other common gin botanicals like anise, coriander, fennel and caraway. Generally considered to be native to the Middle East, it grows wild near rivers in cool climates such as the UK and Scandina. It is also cultivated in France, Belgium and Germany.

Angelica root is dried and shredded before use and adds a slightly piney dry, earthy note that is synonymous with classic gin styles. One writer describes it as "putting the dryness into dry gin." In addition to botanicals like orris root, it works as a fixative to help to marry the flavors of other botanicals together. Angelica seed, which is much less commonly used in gin than the root, has a slight musky, floral character that works well with juniper and also with orange.

In addition to flavoring gin, it is often used to flavor various vermouths and liqueurs, such as Chartreuse and Bénédictine. It is also a common ingredient in Aquavits. The roots and leaves are also used by some peoples for their purported medical benefits as a traditional cold remedy.

CITRUS

A whole host of citrus fruits are used as gin botanicals and they play an important part in maintaining the balance of flavor in many gins. The most typical fruits used are lemon and sweet or bitter orange, although others, such as lime, white and pink grapefruit, pomelo, tangerine and even Buddha's Hand, are growing in popularity, especially with craft distillers.

Citrus can be grown globally in warm, sunny climates, although Spain and Italy are among the world's top growers of oranges and lemons. Oranges and Grapefruits from Florida are also popular with American distillers. Typically, the fruits are skinned and the rind left to dehydrate in warm dry air. The dried rind is the primary manner in which citrus is added as a botanical to gin. Citrus fruits and juices are also important ingredients in tonic waters and many gin-based cocktails.

green cardamom flower and pods

CITRUS FRUITS IN GIN

Distillery	Spirit	Citrus
Camelite Distillery	GinSelf Gin	Tangerine
Langley Distillery	Botanic Gin	Tangerine & Buddah's Hand
13th Colony Distillery	Southern Gin	Lime
Tanqueray-Gordons	Tanqueray Rangpur	Rangpur Lime
Distillery Botanica	Moore's Dry Gin	Queensland Wild Lime
St. George Distillery	Botanivore Gin	Bergamot Orange
Dancing Pines Distillery	Dancing Pines Gin	White Grapefruit
Leopold Brothers	Leopold's American Gin	Pomelo

ORRIS ROOT

Orris root is a collective term for the roots of *iris germanica*, *iris pallida* and *iris florentina*. It is the last of these that is most commonly used in gin production. For gin, it is primarily sourced from Southern France, Northern Italy and Morocco, although it can grow throughout the Mediterranean, Northern Africa and parts of India.

The root comes in a powdered form and, by the time it is ready to be used in gin, it has already grown for three to four years. In the Autumn, it is harvested and then dried for two years, which allows the fragrance to intensify. Although orris root can be as young as three or four years old, the most complex and intense flavors come from roots that are five to six years old.

Orris has a subtle, bitter-sweet, floral flavor, which reminds some people of violets or raspberries. In gin, however, it is used to fix or bind the other botanical flavors together. It is used in the same way by perfumers and in the production of potpourri. Sometimes orris root is used as a substitute for jasmine; and it is included in some talcum powders, especially those for the face. In traditional medicine, orris root was used as an anti-inflammatory, and to treat cold symptoms; today, it is frequently used in natural toothpastes.

CARDAMOM

Cardamom is the third most expensive spice in the world after saffron and vanilla. Its cultivation is extremely slow and labor intensive, which is part of what contributes to its cost. The seeds come from the fruits of the cardamom plant, which take three years to mature before they can be harvested. Then the fruits must undergo a labor intensive drying and curing process before and their seeds can go to market and be used in gin production. The seeds are used to add a spiced note to gins reminiscent of ginger, with a little cinnamon and nutmeg as well as a fresh fragrant character that is unique to the spice. Cardamom is related to ginger and while there are different types of cardamom, *Elettaria cardamomum* also known as green cardamom, is the variety usually used in gin. Given the intensity of cardamom's flavor, it is used sparingly in gin production. Gins noted for their use of cardamom are: Plymouth, Boodles, Warner Edwards and BIG Gin.

Native to the Himalayan Mountains, the cultivation of cardamom has spread around the world; with India and Guatemala producing the largest quantities of the spice. While cardamom seeds are the primary way that it is used, its oil is also used in perfumes. Beyond gin, cardamom is popular in Middle Eastern and Indian cooking as well as Scandinavian baking. Cardamom is also a common cultural medicine of Southern Asia, used for throat, skin and stomach ailments.

CINNAMON/CASSIA

Cinnamon and cassia bark are two very closely-related botanicals of the genus *cinnamomum*, which both come from the bark of evergreen trees in tropical and subtropical regions. Native to Southeast Asia, its cultivation is still primarily located in its native regions. While there are several different species of cinnamon available commercially on the spice market, each with a different flavor profile, most cinnamon and cassia in gin is likely of the *Cinnamomum Verum* or *Cinnamomum Cassia* varieties. Other species, specifically Indonesian cinnamon and Vietnamese cinnamon are often sold under the title "cinnamon." So if a distiller says that cinnamon appears in their gin, it could be any one of these four primary species, or perhaps one of the 300 less common species.

All of the botanicals in the cinnamon family can be used in either their dried bark or powdered forms, although the former is favored by distillers. Both forms add spicy, warm notes to a gin that work well alongside nutmeg, orange and cardamom. However, generalizing the flavor of cinnamon and how it manifests itself in gin can be somewhat of a challenge, as we are dealing with several distinct plants, each with their own individual flavor profiles. Therefore we will briefly overview the four main varieties of cinnamon.

TRUE CINNAMON OR SRI LANKA CINNAMON
(Cinnamomum verum)

Predominantly coming from Sri Lanka (formerly Ceylon), cinnamon has been a popular spice for thousands of years and was often used in perfume. It has a sweet yet warm and spicy flavor, that is more delicate than cassia. Because of this it is the preferred cinnamon for desserts and it is much more expensive than the common Chinese cinnamon.

CASSIA OR CHINESE CINNAMON
(Cinnamomum cassia)

It has a similar, yet bolder and sweeter, taste than true cinnamon. Although a native of China, it grows in most Asian countries. In the United States, if you were to buy cinnamon at your local supermarket, odds are this is the kind of cinnamon that you are getting.

INDONESIAN CINNAMON
(Cinnamomum Burmannii)

Perhaps the second most common kind of cinnamon, Indonesian Cinnamon is occasionally marketed in the United States as just "cinnamon." It has the lowest oil content and it is considered to be the mildest of all of the major types of cinnamon.

VIETNAMESE CINNAMON
(Cinnamomum Laureiroi)

It has more essential oils than any of the other major varieties and has the strongest flavor. It is considered to be spicier than the other varieties, lacking in the delicate sweetness of the popular Sri Lankan Cinnamon. Beyond gin, cinnamon is used in a wide range of culinary purposes: from curries and meat dishes, to drinks, desserts and pastries. It has also been used in traditional medicine to relieve upset stomachs or cold symptoms.

LICORICE ROOT

Typically used in its powdered form, licorice root provides sweetness and its distinctive flavor to a gin. Its flavor is often described as being similar to anise or fennel, but it is in fact not botanically related to either of these plants. Licorice as a sweetener is among the most potent natural sweetening agents. In fact, licorice was often the sweetener of choice for botanically-sweetened Old Tom Gins. Licorice has been used as a sweetener for hundreds of years, long before the advent of sugar plantations, and its sweetening power is 30-50 times greater than sucrose, or table sugar. Its intense sweetness is due to the presence of glycyrrhizin, which differs from sugar in the way that the sweetness slowly builds and lingers.

Like juniper and many other common gin botanicals, licorice is a hardy plant native to the Mediterranean region, though it grows throughout Central Asia, China and a few places in Southern California. Licorice roots requires several seasons of growth to reach a maturity and size large enough to be profitable. But once a plant is fully grown, the roots can extend up to four feet below the surface. Mature licorice is harvested in the autumn, by digging up the roots before the frost.

Other popular uses for licorice are in the manufacture of confectionery and in tobacco blending. Medicinally, it has been a traditional remedy used to treat cold symptoms, toothache and indigestion. Today, it is a popular ingredient in modern cough syrups, due to its sweetness.

A graphic showing popular botanicals used in gin,
the larger the text, the more prevalent the botanical.

Chapter Four

On Tasting Gin

Whilst there are myriad great craft gins made in the United States and beyond, we can only fit so many in the book so here is a selection of note-worthy gins from the US, UK and the wider world. For details on other gins, check out www.craftofgin.com for updates. Also, for these tasting notes Angelica refers to Angelica Root, Coriander to Coriander Seed, Cilantro to Coriander Leaf, Orris to Orris Root and when referring to citrus fruits it is a reference to their peels.

US CRAFT GIN

Listed alphabetically by state and distillery

BRANDON'S GIN (46.0% ABV)

Rock Town Distillery
Little Rock, Arkansas
www.arkansaslightning.com
Base: New Make Red Winter Wheat Spirit.
Botanicals: Juniper, Coriander, Angelica, Lemon, Orange, Cinnamon, and Anise.
Nose: Juniper, with spice, lemon and coriander.
Taste: Smooth and complex with many layers. Lots of spicy pepper notes from sweet pepper to sharper peppery notes. A gin that takes it's own path with some nuttiness, leafy herbalism and soapy coriander. Finishing up with candied lemon and caramel.

JUNIPERO GIN (49.3% ABV)
Anchor Distilling
San Francisco, California
www.anchordistilling.com
Base: Neutral Grain Spirit.
Botanicals: Juniper, Coriander, Licorice and at least ten secret botanicals.
Nose: Juniper, coriander and sweet citrus.
Taste: Strong, fresh, green "fir-like", resiny thick juniper. Rich mouthfeel that coats the palate and surprisingly smooth for it's near 100 Proof strength. Some spicy citrus with ample depth with coriander and lemon; relatively classic with a slight twist. Vibrant and lively.

ST. GEORGE DRY RYE GIN (45.0% ABV)
St. George Spirits
Alameda, California
www.stgeorgespirits.com
Base: Rye Spirit.
Botanicals: Juniper, Caraway, Grapefruit, Lime, Black Peppercorn.
Nose: Malty and peppery, distinct notes of caraway. Calls to mind "rye bread" or a good Scandinavian aquavit.
Taste: Smooth, slightly oily texture. Warm and malty like white dog whiskey which is followed by complex notes of juniper, orange rind, herbal menthol and a touch of berry on the long finish.

LEOPOLD'S AMERICAN SMALL BATCH GIN (40.0% ABV)
Leopold Brothers Distillery
Denver, Colorado
www.leopoldbros.com
Base: New make spirit made from Barley, Wheat, Potato.
Botanicals: Juniper, Coriander, Orange, Orris, Cardamom, Pomelo.
Nose: Very fresh, with some leafy notes akin to fleshy vegetables like cucumber. Floral and dusky herbs, too.
Taste: Floral, with a hint of fresh salad and herbs. Slightly sweet, but with a dry edge from the piney juniper, reminiscent of eastern European gins.

ROUNDHOUSE GIN (47.0% ABV)
Roundhouse Spirits
Boulder, Colorado
www.roundhousespirits.com
Base: Neutral Grain Spirit.
Botanicals: Juniper, Coriander, Citrus Peel, Star Anise, Angelica, and Orris;

Hints of Sencha Green Tea, Lavender, Hibiscus and Chamomile blossoms.
Nose: Warm and a bit junipery, hint of summer flowers.
Taste: Clean and smooth to start; flavors of anise and fennel, almost pastis-like, then juniper and soft chamomile. More floral notes moving towards lavender. On the finish the taste fades to soft juniper and pine.

DOGFISH HEAD JIN (40.0% ABV)
Dogfish Head Brewery & Distillery
Rehoboth Beach, Delaware
www.dogfish.com
Base: New Make Spirit made from Barley, Corn, and Rye.
Botanicals: Juniper, Black Peppercorn, Hops, Cucumber.
Nose: Bright juniper with a touch of sweetness and herbal pickle notes.
Taste: Spicy and warm with plenty of juniper and hint of lavender and some malty hops notes. The flavor then moves on to a more savory character with mild vegetal notes, lingering cucumber and a distinct peppercorn spice on the finish.

SOUTHERN GIN (41.2% ABV)
Thirteenth Colony Distillery
Americus, Georgia
www.13colony.net
Base: Neutral Grain Spirit (predominantly corn).
Botanicals: Juniper, Angelica, Lemon, Orange, Licorice, Anise, Cloves, Lime, Lavender, Cucumber & seven others that remain a mystery.
Nose: Complex and inviting with punchy, but not overwhelming pine.
Taste: Sweet rosemary followed by warm pine and Douglas-fir. More leafy herbal than spicy with a deep flavor, plenty to explore. The finish brings a little heat along with some lime.

BARDENAY LONDON DRY GIN (47.1% ABV)
Bardenay Restaurant & Distillery
Boise, Idaho
www.bardenay.com
Base: Neutral Grain Spirit.
Botanicals: Juniper, Coriander, Lemon, Orange, Orris, Cinnamon, Nutmeg, Lime, Anise, Grapefruit, Caraway, and Mint.
Nose: Strong and junipery, inviting with a bit of alcohol vapor.
Taste: Creamy and thick mouthfeel. Citrus and vanilla immediately present themselves. "Warm spice lemon," and "crisp juniper." Brief punctuating heat that fades quickly. Refreshing finish.

FEW AMERICAN GIN (40.0% ABV)

FEW Spirits Distillery
Evanston, Illinois
www.fewspirits.com
Base: High Corn White Whiskey: 70% Corn, 20% Wheat, 10% 2 Row Malt.
Botanicals: 11 botanicals including: Juniper, Lemon, Orange, Grains of Paradise,
Vanilla and Cascade Hops.
Nose: Notes of wheat, grain, malt and wood come through predominantly,
making this reminiscent of a whiskey (the base of the gin really comes through).
These are followed by some pine, citrus and a touch of coriander.
Taste: Very soft and smooth initially, with a notable sweetness like licorice or
meringue with burnt peaks. The taste is complex, with more traditional gin notes
of pine, lemon and coriander accompanied by creamy vanilla, floral notes and
hints of chocolate. The finish is very long and dry, but full of anise and licorice; it
contrasts with the earlier sweetness to be almost bitter and palate cleansing.

PROHIBITION GIN (40.0% ABV)

Heartland Distillers
Indianapolis, Indiana
www.prohibitiongin.com
Base: Corn (Indiana Vodka).
Botanicals: Juniper, Coriander, Angelica, Licorice, Cinnamon, and a mystery
botanical.
Nose: Soft juniper and vanilla with a hint of lemon sherbert.
Taste: Quite soft to start with a fair bit of sweetness coming from licorice and
anise as well as a hint of cinnamon spice this then moves to sweet black licorice
with a hint of spicy coriander and then some dry piney juniper. A thick finish of
black licorice mixed with pine An intriguing combination of sweet and savory.

RIVER ROSE GIN (40.0% ABV)

Mississippi River Distilling Company
Le Claire, Iowa
www.mrdistilling.com
Base: Corn Spirit.
Botanicals: Juniper, Coriander, Angelica, Lemon, Orange, Cardamom,
Cinnamon, Anise, Lavender, Grapefruit, Cucumber, and Rose Petals.
Nose: Sweet and spicy, hints of Christmas cookies, caraway, coriander and leafy
lemon.
Taste: Bold caraway moving to citrus (bright lemonade) with some floral hints.
The juniper then pops up bitter and dry. A long, gentle fresh finish of anise and
cucumber.

MOST WANTED GIN (40.0% ABV)

High Plains Distillery
Atchison, Kansas
www.highplainsinc.com
Base: Neutral Grain Spirit (from corn).
Botanicals: Juniper, Orange, Anise and Fennel.
Nose: Straight-forward with juniper and citrus (predominantly grapefruit).
Taste: Citrus to start with lemon and sweet orange. Lots of power behind the flavor and the juniper dominates the middle, this leads way to a touch of sherbert and then a slightly sour finish. The gin is smooth through-out with a little power and heat building toward the end.

CORSAIR GIN (46.0% ABV)

Corsair Distillery
Bowling Green, Kentucky
www.corsairartisan.com
Base: Neutral Grain Spirit.
Botanicals: 12 to 14 botanicals including Juniper, Coriander, Orange, Lemon, Orris and Angelica.
Nose: Complex and herbal, has an almost "broth like" or "warm minestrone soup" character. A little bit of citrus on the edges. Inviting and unique.
Taste: Juniper comes out on the taste, along with a host of herbal notes; rosemary, oregano, bay leaf, thyme, tea, and celery combining to give a general vegetal character. Some hints of lemon and bitter citrus rind and a peppery tail and long finish.

CRATER LAKE GIN (47.5% ABV)

Bendistillery
Bend, Oregon
www.bendistillery.com
Base: Neutral Grain Spirit.
Botanicals: Juniper (*juniperus occidentalis*).
Nose: A bit harsh, lots of heat and alcohol burn but a slight note of fresh juniper.
Taste: Still bit of harshness, but a juniper lover's delight. Bright and fresh, nothing short of "vibrant" and "vivacious" with a hint of vanilla in the middle. Fresh juniper lingers in the heat of the finish giving it a vegetable, "cucumber-like" character. Adding juniper via infusion reveals a much more complex berry than you usually get in a gin.

AVIATION AMERICAN GIN (42.0% ABV)
House Spirits
Portland, Oregon
www.aviationgin.com
Base: Neutral Grain Spirit.
Botanicals: Juniper, Coriander, Angelica, Orange, Cardamom, Lavender, and Sarsaparilla Root.
Nose: Menthol, spearmint, dark chocolate, savory, salty and a hint of cardamom.
Taste: Herbal and salty to start, with some warmth. It grows bitter towards the end, being earthy, with hints of burnt toast, wood, resin and salted butter. In the middle of the flavor profile, there's some piney juniper. Finally, a warm finish with floral notes.

INGENIUM GIN (47.0% ABV)
New England Distillers
Portland, Maine
www.newenglanddistilling.com
Base: New Make Malted Barley Spirit.
Botanicals: Ten botanicals including Juniper, Lemon Peel, Lemongrass, and Rose Flower.
Nose: Rich and earthy, coriander. Spicy and a bit of heat.
Taste: Again, rich and earthy: coriander and angelica. Malty with a warm genever like character. Lemongrass and white pepper on the finish. Vaguely exotic tasting. Warm and well balanced.

BLACK RIVER GIN (43.0% ABV)
Sweetgrass Winery & Distillery
Union, Maine
www.sweetgrasswinery.com
Base: Neutral Grain Spirit.
Botanicals: Seven botanicals including Juniper and Blueberries.
Nose: Sweet and contemporary style with cassia, cinnamon and a touch of licorice which give the impression of talcum powder. Some citrus fruit and vanilla sweetness too.
Taste: Mellow sweetness, hints of berry. Rich and luxurious, thick bouquet of floral notes, blueberry pie. Juniper on the tail, heat on the finish with a lingering juniper note.

GALE FORCE GIN (44.4% ABV)
Triple Eight Distillery
Nantucket, Massachusetts

www.ciscobrewers.com/distillery
Base: Organic Wheat Spirit.
Botanicals: Juniper, Lemon, Orange, Cassia, Star Anise, Lemongrass, Mint, and
Lemon Verbena.
Color: Light straw-yellow.
Nose: Confectionery with hints of vanilla and lemon candy offset by earthy
undertones.
Taste: Soft to start, then juniper cream, intense lemon and orange, this fades to a
flash of spice, such as cinnamon and a finish of black peppercorn and dry juniper.

KNICKERBOCKER GIN (42.5% ABV)

New Holland Brewing & Distilling
Holland, Michigan
www.newhollandbrew.com
Base: Neutral Grain Spirit.
Botanicals: Juniper, Coriander, Angelica, Lemon, Orange, Orris, Cinnamon,
Caraway, Cloves, Nutmeg, Fennel, and Ginger.
Nose: Clean lemon rind, sharp juniper, a bit of heat and a touch of cardamom.
Taste: Flavorful and intense citrus and juniper followed by intricate weave of
spices including cinnamon, cassia nutmeg and coriander; this warmth is followed
by a dry finish.

BRISTOW GIN (47.0% ABV)

Cathead Distillery
Jackson, Mississippi
www.bristowgin.com
Base: Cathead Vodka (made from corn).
Botanicals: Hyssop, Cinnamon, Juniper, Orange Peels, Clove, plus six proprietary
botanicals.
Nose: Subtle juniper and citrus, with a touch of floral coriander charm.
Taste: Initially spicy coriander and then a predominant flavor of juniper rounded
by some earthy notes. Then there is citrus peel, more coriander and spicy
cardamom.

PINCKNEY BEND AMERICAN GIN (46.5% ABV)

Pinckney Bend Distillery
New Haven, Missouri
www.pinckneybend.com
Base: Corn Spirit.
Botanicals: Juniper, Coriander, Angelica, Orris, Licorice, Lavender, and three
different Citrus Peels.

Nose: Strong, sweet juniper, hints of dark chocolate and orange.

Taste: Smooth initially with cinnamon and a building peppery warmth. This quickly clears to leave a refreshing lemon/orange note complimented by the juniper. Lots of citrus and spicy black pepper on the finish.

SILVERTIP AMERICAN DRY GIN (44.0% ABV)

Ridge Distillery
Kalispell, Montana
www.ridgedistillery.com
Base: Neutral Grain Spirit.
Botanicals: Juniper, Coriander, Angelica, Orris, and Caraway.
Nose: Soft, savory and spicy with bright juniper and a hint of anise.
Taste: Soft and smooth with some bitter earthy, savory notes. Spiced orange, angelica, coriander and dry orris. An earthy spicy finish with dry cinnamon and licorice.

KARNER BLUE GIN (44.0% ABV)

Flag Hill Winery & Distillery
Lee, New Hampshire
www.flaghill.com
Base: Apple Spirit.
Botanicals: Nine botanicals including Juniper, Lemon, Orange, Orris and Cinnamon.
Nose: Sweet, floral and rich. Apricot jam and blackberry with a touch of cardamom and luxurious lemon pie.
Taste: Smooth and cream to start, growing depth with spice and bitter orange reminiscent of gingerbread and green pepper jam.

GLORIOUS GIN (45.0% ABV)

Breuckelen Distilling
Brooklyn, New York
www.brkdistilling.com
Base: New Make New York Wheat Spirit.
Botanicals: Juniper, Lemon, Rosemary, Ginger, and Grapefruit.
Nose: Musky, with warm sweetness, like that of honey, and hints of cinnamon. This is followed by powerful citrus: lemon, orange and even a faint intimation of grapefruit. Fresh and vibrant, but decidedly not gin-like at first sniff.
Taste: Smooth, light and citrus-forward. The rosemary flavor is definitely there, though I wouldn't have called it out. Breuckelen's gin has a "fresh" and "herbal" flavor, but myriad different herbs appear at points: thyme, lavender, and sage all come to mind. The finish is long and dry, with notes of savory cinnamon, ginger

and light pepper, accompanied by bitter orange and lemon.

FARMER'S BOTANICAL GIN (46.7% ABV)
Crop Harvest Earth Company
New York, New York
www.farmersgin.com
Base: Organic Grain Spirit (distilled in Minnesota).
Botanicals: Juniper, Coriander, Angelica, Elderflower, Lemongrass and a number of undisclosed botanicals.
Nose: Juniper with coriander and some faint floral notes
Taste: Orange and citrusy, with a bright sweetness of elderflower. Compliments the dryness of the juniper nicely. Not overwhelmingly floral, but finishes with a lingering floral burn bringing with it notes of lemongrass, juniper and a bit more elderflower.

GREENHOOK GIN (47.0%ABV)
Greenhook Ginsmiths
Brooklyn, New York
www.greenhookgin.com
Base: Organic New York Wheat Spirit.
Botanicals: Juniper, Coriander, Citrus, Orris, Chamomile, Elderflower, Elderberry, Thai Blue Ginger, and Ceylon Cinnamon.
Nose: Non-traditional with light smoke, spice and orris as well as a hint of chamomile.
Taste: Elderflower at first, but quickly offset with a crisp earthy note of coriander. Unsweetened cinnamon and an almost galanga like heat. Dry and complex finish with very little heat.

DOROTHY PARKER GIN (44.0% ABV)
New York Distilling
Brooklyn, New York
www.nydistilling.com
Base: Neutral Grain Spirit (from corn).
Botanicals: Juniper, Lemon, Orange, Cardamom, Cinnamon, Elderberries and Hibiscus Petals.
Nose: Refreshing, slightly sweet floral notes such as hibiscus. These are accompanied by a lemon and passion-fruit fruitiness, coriander seed and green juniper.
Taste: Full of classic gin flavors and superbly balanced throughout. Strong start with notes of juniper and spice, like cassia, followed by a plethora of both sweet and slightly sour fruity notes: candied orange, grapefruit, lemon and elderberry as

well as some floral (lavender and hibiscus) notes. The finish is light with lemon, orange and the slight warmth of raw savory cinnamon.

COMB9 GIN (47.0% ABV)
StilltheOne Distillery
Port Chester, New York
www.combvodka.com
Base: New Make Honey Spirit.
Botanicals: Juniper, Coriander, Licorice, Lavender, Rose, Citrus Peel, Galangal Root, plus two mystery botanicals.
Nose: Sweet soft and rich with a slight muskiness.
Taste: Much stronger than the nose, with juniper and good fresh flashes of citrus peppered with spice throughout. A strong, long and dry finish of lingering juniper and lightly acidic lemon.

CARDINAL GIN (42.0% ABV)
Southern Artisan Spirits
Kings Mountain, North Carolina
www.southernartisanspirits.com
Base: Neutral Grain Spirit.
Botanicals: Juniper, Coriander, Angelica, Orange, Orris, Cardamom, Grains of Paradise, Cloves, Frankincense, Spearmint, and Apricot Kernels.
Nose: Juniper with some floral notes and a hint of heathland
Taste: A little heat to start followed by a mix of sweet winter spice (clove, cinnamon, nutmeg) and a hint of sarsaparilla. A long lingering spearmint finish.

BLUECOAT AMERICAN DRY GIN (47.0%ABV)
Philadelphia Distillery
Philadelphia, Pennsylvania
www.philadelphiadistilling.com
Base: Spirit made from a mix of Corn, Wheat, Rye, and Barley.
Botanicals: Juniper, Coriander, Angelica, Lemon, Navel and Valencia Orange.
Nose: Bright, bracing citrus. Lots of orange, hints of lemon and other sweet citrus fruits such as grapefruit. Also a slight creaminess.
Taste: An intense gin with juniper up front followed by warm spicy orange. The gin is packed full of fresh zesty citrus and this gives way to a more confection citrus like a rich and creamy lemon sponge. Definitely a gin, but citrus dominates the palate the entire way through.

WHITE TIGER GIN (45.0% ABV)
Dark Corner Distillery

Greenville, South Carolina
www.darkcornerdistillery.com
Base: Corn Spirit.
Botanicals: Thai Basil, Juniper, Jasmine, Szechuan Peppercorn, and Lemongrass.
Nose: Smells instantly gin like, but still rather subtle. A faint note of black pepper. Understated, but primarily juniper-like. Hints of heat too.
Taste: The taste is distinctly contemporary in character. A little bit oily on the lips, juniper and peppercorn start out, but the heat and power of the botanicals rise rather quickly. There's a crescendo where a lot of things are happening all at once. A note of black pepper and juniper flares suddenly against the backdrop of moonshine, you get a bit of a traditional gin taste, some coriander and earthy notes, combined with bright lemongrass and a muted floral character. The heat is rather intense here. It fades then, lingering hot in the back of the mouth, a little bit sour with perhaps a hint of citrus and some more of that peppercorn note and just a hint of a malty, woodsy aftertaste.

WATERLOO GIN (47.0% ABV)

Treaty Oak Distilling
Austin, Texas
treatyoakdistilling.blogspot.com
Base: Wheat Spirit.
Botanicals: Juniper, Coriander, Angelica, Lemon, Orange, Licorice, Grapefruit, Lavender, Ginger, Rosemary, and Pecan.
Nose: Warm juniper and a little bit of heat and sweet spiciness.
Taste: Distinctive and crammed full of flavor with some sweetness. Rosemary and nopal up front with hints of demerara sugar and toasted pecan. Juniper is strong throughout with some orange and root beer.

WATERSHED GIN (50.0% ABV)

Catoctin Creek Distillery
Purcellville, Virginia
www.catoctincreekdistilling.com
Base: Organic Rye Spirit.
Botanicals: Ten botanicals including Juniper, Coriander, Cinnamon, Anise and Citrus.
Nose: The nose is a tad straw like, with hints of grain and cereal and a little vanilla as well as an oily citrus note with hints of hibiscus and blueberry. Very subtly floral, but predominantly grainy.
Taste: Smooth thick and syrupy with juniper and a hint of cassia upfront then some slightly floral sweetness from the rye. Engaging with a great depth of flavor and some savory almost salty elements. Citrus in the middle some earthy woody notes leading to a long spicy finish.

BARR HILL GIN (45.0% ABV)
Caledonia Spirits & Winery
Hardwick, Vermont
www.caledoniaspirits.com
Base: New Make Corn Spirit.
Botanicals: Juniper and Honey.
Color: Given the honey infusion, the gin has a light straw color.
Nose: Full of complexity and subtleties, juniper and beeswax.
Taste: Plenty of fresh, green and piney juniper followed by a hint of rose. The complex honey sweetness is reminiscent of Turkish delight or honey and juniper candy. The finish is a combination of the two with fresh pine and beeswax. Incredible.

BIG GIN (47.0% ABV)
Captive Spirits Distillery
Ballard, Washington
www.captivespiritsdistilling.com
Base: Neutral Grain Spirit.
Botanicals: Juniper, Coriander, Angelica, Bitter Orange, Grains of Paradise, Cassia, Cardamom, Orris, and Tasmanian Pepperberry.
Nose: Strong and assertive, juniper, followed by zesty lemon and a hint of pepper and cardamom spice.
Taste: BIG thick and silky, with bright burst of juniper. the gin has many classic elements but the strength of the flavors gives it a slight contemporary air. Citrus, spice and floral sweetness, akin to fresh cut orange or bouquet of flowers. Simply excellent.

GREEN HAT GIN (40.7% ABV)
New Columbia Distillers
Washington D.C
www.greenhatgin.com
Base: New Make Soft Red Winter Wheat Spirit.
Botanicals: Juniper, Coriander, Angelica, Orris, Lemon, Grapefruit, Cassia Bark, Fennel, Sage, Grains of Paradise, Lemongrass, and Celery Seed.
Nose: The nose is very floral, very pronounced. Notes of juniper, lemon and a bright almost jammy sweetness.
Taste: Very, very smooth. Crisp citrus flavor at first, very clear, hints of lemon and orange and a bright floral note. The flavors begin to shift to a rich earthy base with the juniper hovering in the background. The finish is clean with very little heat and ends in the floral notes of summer fields, lavender, marigold, elderflower and finally a note of celery salt.

GREENBRIER GIN (40.0% ABV)

Smooth Ambler Spirits

Maxwelton, West Virginia

www.smoothambler.com

Base: Whitewater Vodka (made from corn, wheat & barley).

Botanicals: Juniper, Coriander, Angelica, Lemon, Orange, Cardamom, and Black Pepper.

Nose: Warm and nutty, slightly malty; reminiscent of genever. Some citrus on the nose, grapefruit and coriander. Warm, inviting, and a bit sweet.

Taste: Juniper and citrus in nice harmony. Peppery and bright, with earthy notes from coriander. Middle has a bright malty spice with ginger and cinnamon. Long and smooth finish. Complex and well rounded.

DEATH'S DOOR GIN (47.0% ABV)

Death's Door Spirits

Middleton, Wisconsin

www.deathsdoorspirits.com

Base: Spirit made from Washington Island Wheat & Malted Barley from Chilton, Wisconsin.

Botanicals: Juniper, Coriander, and Fennel.

Nose: Juniper, citrus and some earthy fennel.

Taste: Well-rounded and balanced; juniper up front then spicy coriander with complex fennel and anise, not as sweet. Smooth and some small hints of chocolate.

REHORST GIN (44.0% ABV)

Great Lakes Distillery

Milwaukee, Wisconsin

www.greatlakesdistillery.com

Base: Neutral Grain Spirit.

Botanicals: Nine botanicals including Sweet Basil and Wisconsin Ginseng

Nose: A quiet nose with a hint of citrus and juniper and a tiny hint of mint.

Taste: Complex, the basil and herbal notes give off some Pesto notes along with a bracing and resiny juniper. Other classic flavors of coriander, angelica and citrus are there too. The flavors build to a crescendo and finish as they begun, with basil. An exciting gin that will appeal to traditionalists and trailblazers alike.

UK CRAFT GIN

Listed alphabetically by County and Distillery

DR. J'S GIN (45.0% ABV)

English Spirit Distillery

Dullingham, Cambridgeshire
www.englishvodkacompany.com
Base: New Make Cambridgeshire Sugar Cane Spirit.
Botanicals: Includes five varieties of Coriander.
Nose: Fruity nose, quite floral and with a savory hint. Plenty of coriander, some vanilla reminding me of lemon shortbread.
Taste: Spicy coriander up front with some floral notes. Some green savory soupy notes followed by citrus and a spicy sweetness. Pine and lemon on finish, complex with a perfumed quality.

WILLIAMS GREAT BRITISH GIN (40.0% ABV)

Chase Distillery
Hereford, Herefordshire
www.chasedistillery.co.uk
Base: New Make Potato Spirit.
Botanicals: Juniper, Coriander, Angelica, Lemon, Licorice, Cassia, Almond, Clove, and Cardamom.
Nose: Dry juniper with zesty citrus (orange) and then some warm, spicy notes, making this complex and full.
Taste: Juniper to start and some dark, bitter chocolate and citrus zest. This is followed by warm, spicy notes of cinnamon, nutmeg and ginger.

MASTER OF MALT ORIGIN GIN (BULGARIA) (44.0% ABV)

Master of Malt Distillery
Tunbridge Wells, Kent
www.masterofmalt.com
Part of Master of Malt's Origin Range explore the terroir of juniper and how the flavor of Juniperus Communis varies depending on where it is grown. Currently containing six products with juniper from Netherlands, Italy, Albania, Macedonia, Kosovo and Bulgaria.
Base: Neutral Grain Spirit.
Botanicals: Juniper from Veliki Preslav, Bulgaria.
Nose: Mild and slightly junipery. Not a lot of heat, inviting but sedate.
Taste: Surprisingly floral, although only juniper is among the botanicals hints of rose, hibiscus and "summer fields," amidst the gentle bristle of bright juniper. Fresh, medium length tail, juniper lingering brightly on the edges of the palette. Smooth, quite drinkable.

C.O.L.D. GIN (40.0% ABV)

City of London Distillery
London
www.cityoflondondistillery.com

Base: Neutral Grain Spirit.
Botanicals: Juniper, Coriander, Angelica, Licorice, Lemon, Orange, and Lime.
Nose: Plenty of creamy citrus, a bit like lemon curd as well as juniper and coriander.
Taste: Smooth and well rounded with juniper, coriander, citrus and a hint of raisin at the end. Very well balanced and plenty of citrus with a slightly sweet lift at the end.

SACRED GIN (47.0% ABV)

Sacred Spirits Company
Highgate, London
www.sacredspiritscompany.com
Base: 100% Wheat Neutral Grain Spirit.
Botanicals: Juniper, Coriander, Angelica, Lemon, Orange, Lime, Cardamom, Licorice, Orris, Cassia Bark, Nutmeg, Frankincense and two mystery botanicals.
Nose: Juniper, lemon as well as spice and a touch of cardamom.
Taste: Full and rounded flavor with juniper, coriander and then a touch of dry angelica, the middle is herbal and almost savory and the long dry finish of juniper is garnished with cardamom.

SIPSMITH LONDON DRY GIN (41.6% ABV)

Sipsmith Distillery
Hammersmith, London
www.sipsmith.com
Base: Neutral Grain Spirit.
Botanicals: Juniper, Coriander, Angelica, Licorice, Orris, Almond, Cassia, Cinnamon, Orange and Lemon.
Nose: Full with juniper, cedar with citrus following.
Taste: Juniper followed by rich notes of citrus and coriander as well as some angelica. A powerful gin with a long finish. A modern classic.

WARNER EDWARDS HARRINGTON DRY GIN (44.0% ABV)

Warner Edwards Distillery
Harrington, Northamptonshire
www.warneredwards.com
Base: Barley Spirit.
Botanicals: Juniper, Coriander, Angelica, Lemon, Cardamom, Cinnamon, Black Peppercorns, Elderflower and two mystery botanicals.
Nose: Rich juniper mixed well with licorice and a hint of vanilla cream, a well-defined nose with cardamom and coriander towards the end.
Taste: Light, but full to the brim with notes of juniper, coriander and spice from the very beginning. The spice continues throughout, bringing a good warmth and

texture to it, like it had been made with dashes of chili and ginger, before a softer finish of cardamom.

ADNAMS COPPER HOUSE DISTILLED GIN (40.0% ABV)
Adnams Brewery & Distillery
Southwold, Suffolk
www.adnams.co.uk
Base: New Make Malted Barley Spirit.
Botanicals: Juniper, Coriander, Orris, Lemon, Orange, and Hibiscus.
Nose: Savory with plenty of rosemary.
Taste: Smooth, with a straightforward notes of juniper and coriander. Perhaps a little lighter than many classic dry gins, with a distinctive warmth at the end.

ADNAMS FIRST RATE GIN (48.0% ABV)
Adnams Brewery & Distillery
Southwold, Suffolk
www.adnams.co.uk
Base: New Make Spirit made from Wheat, Barley and Oat.
Botanicals: Juniper, Coriander, Orris, Lemon, Orange, Angelica, Licorice, Cardamom, Vanilla, Caraway, Cassia, Thyme, and Fennel.
Nose: Juniper and light vanilla; slightly reminiscent of creamy bubblegum.
Taste: Very silky, with notes of cardamom and spice, but a little light on juniper. This was more complex than their regular gin, with a stronger taste and a finish of cinnamon and licorice.

GILT SINGLE MALT SCOTTISH GIN (40.0%ABV)
Valt Vodka Company
Paisley, Scotland
www.giltgin.com
Base: 100% Malted Barley Spirit.
Botanicals: Juniper, Coriander, Angelica, Lemon, Orange, Orris, licorice, Cardamom, and Cassia.
Nose: Juniper and hints of vanilla and grain. Ever-so-slightly acidic.
Taste: Dry juniper upfront, followed by coriander and then some notes of malt and hops. In the middle, there are some toffee-vanilla notes, followed by notes of citrus, spice and a light, licorice sweetness. The finish is fresh, with lots of citrus and orange.

WORLD GIN

Listed alphabetically by Country and Distillery

MOORE'S VINTAGE DRY GIN (40.0% ABV)

Distillery Botanica
Erina, Australia
www.st-fiacredistillery.com
Base: Neutral Grain Spirit.
Botanicals: Juniper, Coriander, Angelica, Queensland Wild Lime, Cinnamon
Myrtle, Illawarra Plum, and Macadamia Nut.
Nose: Eucalyptus, citrus and some deeper floral notes.
Taste: Unusual, citrus, floral, dried flower petals, earthy, fruity and floral; in short,
flavorful and complex. Notes of limey citrus as well as a hint of vanilla that often
accompanies the flavor. The eucalyptus was still there as was a touch of pine.
Surprising depth of flavor given that it is only 40% ABV.

LEBENSSTERN DRY GIN (43% ABV)

Freihof Distillery
Lustenau, Austria
www.haromex.com/2535,1,Lebensstern.html
Base: Neutral Grain Spirit.
Botanicals: Juniper and other botanicals.
Nose: Lots of rather fruity, jammy notes, with some sweet juniper, pine, apricot
and peach.
Taste: Quite smooth, with plenty of juniper and rich, jammy, fruity flavors,
including peach, raspberry and apricot. Very good.

G'VINE FLORAISON (40.0% ABV)

EWG Spirits
Chevanceaux, Cognac, France
www.g-vine.com
Base: Neutral Grape Spirit.
Botanicals: Juniper, Coriander, Licorice, Cassia bark, Cardamom, Cubeb Berries,
Nutmeg, Ginger, Lime and a grapeview flower infusion.
Nose: Bright and overwhelmingly floral. Hibiscus and sweet fruits.
Taste: The character of the Ugni Blanc Grape base shines through, lending it a
distinct floral character that dominates. Hints of cassia, juniper, coriander, even
notes of licorice come through, with a bright citrus character. That being said, its
taste profile is more akin to a floral vodka than most gins. Although not subtle,
quite delicious in its own right.

THE DUKE MUNICH DRY GIN (45.0% ABV)
The Duke Distillery
Munich, Germany
www.duke-gin.com
Base: Neutral Grain Spirit.
Botanicals: Juniper, Coriander, Angelica, Lemon, Lavender, Ginger, Orange
Blossom, Hops, Malt, Cinnamon Bark, Cubeb Berries, Caraway and one secret
ingredient.
Nose: Fragrant and complex, with notes of cardamom, coriander, pine and
berries, reminiscent of a wooded glade.
Taste: Floral and herbal, with a touch of bitterness. Flavors include cardamom,
pine, wood bark, heavy coriander, violet, chocolate and coffee. Rich, complex and
a lingering finish.

VILNIUS GIN (45.0% ABV)
Obeliai Spirit Distillery
Audronys I, Lithuania
www.degtine.lt/index.php/products/vilnius-gin
Base: Neutral Grain Spirit.
Botanicals: Juniper, Coriander, Orange and Dill Seeds.
Nose: Lemon, orange and pine.
Taste: A classically styled, rather dry gin, with citrus and some earthy herbal
notes, too. A smooth texture and a strong personality, despite the ABV.

VL29 GIN (41.7% ABV)
Van Toor Distillery
Vlaardingen, Netherlands
www.vl92.com
Base: Neutral Grain and Solid Malt Wine.
Botanicals: 14 Botanicals, including Juniper, Angelica, Bitter Orange, Apricot
Stones, and Cilantro.
Nose: Coriander, hint of tea and some malty brown bread with a floral lift.
Taste: Full flavor up front with some plummy jammy notes such as apricot
followed by some tannin tea notes and a touch of sloe, this moves to some more
floral bergamot and coriander notes with a dry juniper finish.

SOUTH GIN (48.2% ABV)
Pacific Dawn Distillery
Auckland, New Zealand
www.southgin.com
Base: Xtra Neutral Spirit (NGS).
Botanicals: Juniper, Coriander, Angelica Leaf, Lemon, Orange, Orris, Gentian

Root, Manuka Berries, and Kawakawa Leaves.

Nose: Juniper, citrus, anise and a slightly fruity, bubblegum quality, as well as a hint of sarsaparilla.

Taste: Very, very smooth and soft, this is one of the smoothest gins that I have tried. There were good notes of juniper, citrus and a sweet earthiness, with more hints of anise and sarsaparilla (the base of root beer). The sweetness reminds me of pastis, such as Ricard or Pernod.

GINSELF (40.0% ABV)
Camelite Winery & Distillery
Benicasim, Castellón, Spain
www.ginself.com
Base: Neutral Grain Spirit.
Botanicals: Juniper, Angelica Seed, Angelica Root, Sweet Orange, Bitter Orange, Lemon, Orange Blossom, Tiger Nut, and Tangerine.
Nose: Juniper, with spicy, floral coriander and zesty, floral orange. There's also a slight, biscuity nuttiness from the angelica.
Taste: With lots of orange blossom upfront, it reminds me of orange shortbread. These notes are followed by lemon, coriander and a finish of dry, floral pine. Smooth, with a little warmth at the end.

NILS OSCAR TÄRNÖ GIN (41.5% ABV)
Tärnö distillery
Nyköping, Sweden
www.dricka.se/sprit/tarno-gin
Base: Organic Grain Spirit.
Botanicals: Juniper, Coriander, Lemon, Cinnamon, Cardamom, and Elderberry.
Nose: Fruity and floral, with jammy berries and a hint of pine.
Taste: Like the nose, jammy and creamy to start but with growing citrus followed by juniper and some more earthy notes. The finish is a mix of sweet berries, strawberry and elderberry garnished with the dryness you would associated with sloe berry.

STUDER ORIGINAL SWISS GIN (40.0% ABV)
Studer Distillery
Luzern, Switzerland
www.distillery.ch
Base: Neutral Grain Spirit.
Botanicals: Juniper, Coriander, Angelica, Ginger, Lemongrass, Lavender, and Ground Cubeb.
Nose: Rich & fruity; sweet & floral.
Taste: Initially soft, then plenty of juniper-pine with some floral notes. The gin

The two copper Pot Stills of the English Spirit Distillery in Cambridgeshire.

has sweetness and herbal not, but little citrus. Finally there are strong flavors of angelica and coriander.

UGANDA WARAGI (40.0% ABV)

East Africa Brewery
Uganda
www.eabl.com/our-brands/spirits-inner#ugandawaragi
Base: Millet Spirit.
Botanicals: Juniper and other unknown botanicals.
Nose: Mild hints of juniper, quiet and smooth, not much heat.
Taste: Again, predominantly juniper. Smooth in character and almost vaguely herbal, but not a lot going on here. Taste much smoother and flatter than most simple gins. More well-suited for mixing than for drinking straight.

A bottle of Bluecoat American Dry Gin.

Chapter Five

Meeting the Makers

We conducted four interviews with distillers in the United States and the United Kingdom. We asked them about their inspiration, both to start a distillery and to produce gin.

ROBERT CASSELL OF PHILADELPHIA DISTILLING

Robert Cassell, the distiller and designer of Bluecoat Gin, from Philadelphia Distilling is a trail-blazer and inspiration for American craft gin and the rise of the contemporary gin style.

Q1 What do you enjoy most about distilling?
Practicing the art of patience, like a golf swing; when making a gin the more patient you are the better the results. I also love the synergy between art and science that distilling has; the recipe is the artsy fluid, but replicating this with consistency is the science.

Q2 What do you enjoy least about distilling?
[After a long, long pause] Not enough time and the inconsistency of mother nature.

Q3 If you weren't distillers what would you like to do?
I used to be a brewer trained in nuclear medicine, but I think I'd opt for farm-
ing – it has the same satisfaction of working with your hands as distilling.

Q4 Apart from your excellent gin, what other products do you plan to make?
Unaged Corn Whiskey, Absinthe, and 101681 Vodka.

Q5 What do you enjoy drinking?
Apart from my own products, I'm quite a fan of soda. If I see someone with
a birch beer, a root beer or orange cream soda I haven't tried – I'll try and
find it.

Q6 What inspired the style of your Gin?
Observation. I noticed that when people ordered gin and tonic they would
squeeze in their lemon or lime wedge before even tasting it; when I would
ask them (hopefully in a non-creepy way) why they said they like more of
"that" in it. The "that" was citrus, people were manipulating their drink into
this direction – which led to Bluecoat.

Q7 What do you think of the Gin Market in 2013?
Some time last year, a newcomer to the micro-distilling gin world (told me)
"I had your company and your brand in my business plan" that was the funni-
est thing to me as I remember when we were writing ours and looking (at) it
and thinking, "Wow. How can you identify your competitive set when there
has been a peak on the bell curve of craft distilling?" It was just so funny to
me. As small producers there might be a chance of pushing each other out of
the shelf space at a retail level but at the same time I can now mention craft
distilling to a distributor or sales rep and they know what I mean. It's far
more of a case of the rising tide raises all ships. Gin is such a unique spirit;
they will all have their own unique flavors. If you take a drink and make it
with four different craft gins, that cocktail is going to taste really different
for each one.

Q8 How did you get into distilling?
I was doing an analysis on a mass spectrometer on a distilled sample of beer,
looking at compounds within it. This analysis peaked my interest into distillation and its processes. I then did a program at Heriot-Watt University in
Edinburgh.

PAUL HLETKO OF FEW SPIRITS
*FEW is based in Evanstown, Illinois, home of the Woman's Christian Temperance
Union and hence often cited as "the birthplace of prohibition." FEW make two*

gins; an American Gin, using a white whisky base, and a Navy Strength Gin bottled at 57% ABV.

Q1 What do you enjoy most about distilling?
I greatly enjoy the creativity and the opportunity to create new, and fun and exciting drinks. It is exceptionally rewarding to come up with new ideas, try the ideas and then celebrate the good ones and laugh at the bad ones. On top of that, it is fantastic to be a part of a new wave of other creative folks!

Q2 What do you enjoy least about distilling?
This one is easy. The paperwork! The paperwork and reporting and all the tedious documents.

Q3 If you weren't distillers what would you like to do?
I have had a long history of working on creative outlets, so if I were not being creative with spirits, I'd be creative elsewhere. At least hopefully!

Q4 Apart from your excellent gin, what other products do you plan to make?
We currently have some whiskeys on the market, including a bourbon and a rye. We have malt whiskey aging that we are looking forward to releasing. We also like to play and invent, so we're working on amaros, grappa, brandies, and more gins and more whiskeys! We take our craft rather seriously, but firmly believe that we need to continue to play with the stills and keep it fun and fresh.

Q5 What do you enjoy drinking?
I enjoy drinking beverages of all types – spirits, beer, coffee. I enjoy sipping on a fine whiskey in the evening, or sharing cocktails with friends.

Q6 What inspired the style of your Gin?
My gins are inspired by trying to zig when others zag. Our FEW American Gin was inspired by attempting to create a whiskey drinkers gin – we use a whiskey base, with many of the botanicals inspired by whiskeys – vanilla and such. Our Standard Issue Gin was inspired as an homage to the classic British naval gins, but with a bit of a different view.

Q7 What do you think of the Gin Market in 2013?
The Gin Market in 2013 is amazing. I don't remember seeing such an explosion of great new gins and opportunity to experience different takes on the great spirit. There are so many great gins on the market now, created by some amazingly talented people. 2013 is the best time to be a gin drinker, for sure!

A bottle of FEW Spirit's American Dry Gin.

Q8 How did you get into distilling?
I started distilling to create new and different spirits. Prior to World War II, my grandfather's family owned a major brewery in what is now the Czech Republic. After the Nazis invaded, they lost the brewery, and my grandfather was the only survivor of the camps. He spent the rest of his life trying to get the brewery back, and when he died, I wanted to build on this family legacy. But I want to build on it by creating something new, rather than just looking to the past.

JOHN WALTERS OF ENGLISH SPIRITS DISTILLERY
In the heart of the sugar beet land in the Cambridgeshire countryside, the English Spirits Distillery is unusual for the UK in that it makes its own base spirit. They also make the only English Rum.

Q1 What do you enjoy most about distilling?
At the end of each still run, you produce a spirit that, before you began, couldn't be bought for any money. The raison d'etre for setting this up was to produce something delicious and that puts smiles on peoples' faces.

Q2 What do you enjoy least about distilling?
Paying vast sums of duty to the government at the same rates as Diageo; there's no concession to micro-distillers in this country.

Q3 If you weren't distillers what would you like to do?
Perfumer; it's closely related to gin making, so it makes perfect sense.

Q4 Apart from your excellent gin, what other products do you plan to make?
Vodka, and a rum (the only one in the UK) that's made from molasses fermented and distilled ourselves and we do recycle the heads and tails, which is very important for rum. We have also just started making malt to distill by using worts from the local microbreweries; they will then age the resulting spirit.

Q5 What do you enjoy drinking?
I'm a big fan of wine fan and the seasonality of spirits. Good wine, good beer and good spirits all have something to offer. I do really like Black Panther Ale from the Panther Brewery in Reepham – it's flawless.

Q6 What inspired the style of your Gin?
I felt that the fashion for cramming the entire Amazon into a gin bottle was a little bit wrong. I felt that, like superb cooking, you can produce incredibly emergent experiences if you finely balance things. Simplicity is massively

A bottle of Warner Edwards Harrington Dry Gin

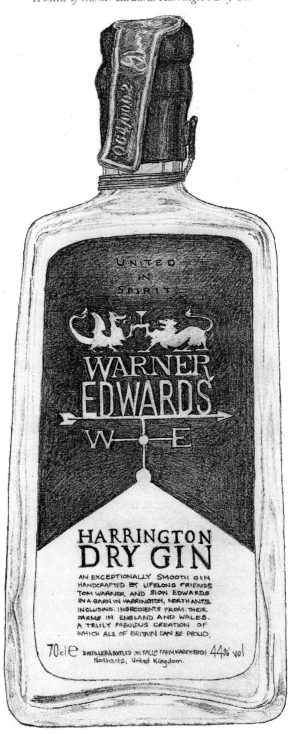

underrated, so we took some simple gears, such as juniper and coriander, and tweaked the bedrock of gin. Coriander has a complexity and sweetness to it, and each of its varieties are broadly different. We wanted to give people the option to choose a very different style of gin, with those different citrus notes – a sunshiny gin. It's a modern take on the classic gin recipe, done to the Nth degree, from farm to sip.

Q7 What difference does it make being in Cambridgeshire?
This is a quiet area, and in the sticks people will prick up their ears, provenance and promoting it. Start off by creating region. The juniper is grown locally and so is the mash for the spirit as we're in the middle of sugar beet country.

Q8 How did you get into distilling?
Listening to a radio program on Eau de Vie. I think Eau de Vie is fantastic and the person on the radio said that it was illegal to make it in the UK, but I knew there had to be something that can be done about that. Today, I'm looking at making it from local grape and carrot growers.

Tom Warner & Sion Edwards of Warner Edwards Distillery
One of the newest craft distilleries in the UK, they distilled their first batch in December 2012. I spoke to owners, distillers, bottlers, Tom Warner and Sion Edwards at their distillery in the village of Harrington in England.

Q1 What do you enjoy most about distilling?
Tom— Creating something for others to enjoy; it is so fulfilling when people try it, enjoy it and smile. I'm making something real.

Sion— When the still is running, it is really exciting, almost magical and tasting the gin off a run – it's the same satisfaction some get from baking.

Q2 What do you enjoy least about distilling?
Tom— Bottling and wrapping the copper around the bottle (it's sharp).

Sion— Actually, I quite like bottling.

Q3 If you weren't distillers what would you like to do?
Tom— International Professional Rugby Player.

Sion— Electrical Engineer.

Q4 Apart from your excellent gin, what other products do you plan to make?
Tom— We're interested in making sloe, damson and elderflower gins using our dry gin.

Sion— As TV chef Keith Floyd once said "if a wine is not good enough to drink don't cook with it." We feel the same about sloe gin.

Q5 What do you enjoy drinking?
Tom— I love to drink gin and real ales; not in the same glass, but I like to start a session on the ale and then move on to gin and tonic. Adnams Broadside is a particular favorite. I think Sion likes strawberry milkshakes.

Sion— I really enjoy to drink Port, good red wine (currently I am favoring Italian wines), continental beers, especially Belgian and German, Vodka (Belvedere) and, of course Gin. I do like Strawberry milkshakes!

Q6 What inspired the style of your Gin?
Tom— Our tastes really inspired the flavor. We wanted something that was strong in the mouth but not overpowering, that could be drunk on its own or work well in cocktails. We went down a relatively spicy route early on when developing the flavor but toned this back as some of the prototypes tasted like liquid curry!

Sion— We had a tasting around the kitchen table following research on a number of already available gins. We like smooth gins and we were attempting to achieve a gin that could be drunk straight and thankfully we achieved it! We felt that if we created a gin that we liked, it would be liked by others.

Q7 What difference does it make being in Harrington?
Tom— Harrington is the epicenter of the universe which is surprising for a village of 100 people. We have a WWII American airbase, a cold war nuclear bunker and the famous Falls Farm where the distillery is located. It's an idyllic setting that helps create and make our gin special. The cons are the fact we do not have a captive local audience like a London based distillery, so it will take longer for us to spread the word, but hopefully the quality of our gin will help to carry the message.

Sion— Harrington is a great location; it's a beautiful village it's not far to most of the UK (or the center of the universe as Tom puts it!), the water is superb, the history is immense and the name Harrington just lends itself to a great Dry Gin!

Q8 How did you get into distilling?
We originally wanted to make essential oil, but then when we saw that you could do something similar and make gin (which we both used to enjoy at college) it was a no-brainer.

Chapter Six

The Gin Cocktail Canon

There are hundreds upon thousands of gin cocktails recipes out there in books, newspapers, and even bartenders' minds. But despite all these concoctions, the beginning gin connoisseur need only be intimately familiar with about seven cocktails. These seven cocktails are usually considered the classics, and several are even considered "official cocktails" by the International Bartenders Association. Our definition is a bit different.

These seven cocktails are so chosen because in knowing these seven drinks, you can make a drink for every kind of taste and every occasion. With these recipes, there will be few gin and non-gin drinkers alike that you will fail to satisfy.

Essential Gin Cocktail #1: The Aviation

The Aviation's origins date back to the 1910's, but unlike many cocktails from that era which have endured, this drink tumbled into an unfortunate limbo. This was because one of the key ingredients: Crème De Violette (a violet flavored liqueur), was actually almost unobtainable for most of the twentieth century.

At this time, the Aviation lived on as a variation of a Tom Collins rather than the elegant floral cocktail it was. Happily, this floral liqueur is back on shelves today and we can once again enjoy the Aviation in it's full, colorful glory.

Best With: Floral and contemporary styled gins like G'vine's Floraison, Seneca Drums, or Back River Gin.

> 4 parts gin
> 1 part Crème De Violette
> 1 part Maraschino
> 1 part fresh squeezed lemon juice
> Shake with ice, strain into a cocktail glass. Serve straight up and garnish with a maraschino cherry.

Essential Gin Cocktail #2: The Gimlet

Rose's Lime Juice has an illustrious and long lived history dating back to its origins as a way of preserving citrus juice in the British Navy. The Gimlet hasn't always been exclusively the domain of Rose's Lime Juice; in fact, early recipes often just used lime. In the present day, if you order a Gimlet you are probably getting gin and Rose's Lime Juice, although Vodka Gimlets are also popular.

A bold gin will stand assertively in this cocktail, but the distinctive sweet and sour tang of Rose's Lime Juice can complement a fine gin. The Gimlet is a strong, flavorful, and very easy to make cocktail. The ratios vary in the literature, so mix to taste. I would recommend the one below as a good starting point.

Best With: A strong classic styled gin, with lots of juniper upfront like Tanqueray or BIG Gin.

> 4 parts gin
> 1 part Rose's Lime Juice (or other lime cordial)
> Shake with ice and strain.

Essential Gin Cocktail #3: The Tom Collins

As one of the cocktails dating back to the esteemed Jerry Thomas and his renowned Bartender's Guide, the Tom Collins has a rather long popular history. This has led to a wide array of subtle variations, for instance swap simple syrup for honey and you have a Bees' Knees. The Tom Collins is a tall sparkling lemonade with gin in it. It is often one of the first gin cocktails people try (the oft served, dive bar "Gin Sour" is essentially a Tom Collins) and a properly made Tom Collins can be one of the best cocktails for introducing new folks to gin.

Best With: Citrus forward gins shine here, especially ones which emphasize orange like Bluecoat, or Plymouth.

> 3 parts gin
> 2 parts rresh squeeze lemon juice
> 2 tsp. simple syrup
> Mix together in a glass with ice, stir, fill glass with soda and serve.

Essential Cocktail #4: The Martini

There are few more controversial cocktails out there than the Martini. The Martini has inspired more mythology, discussion, and variations than any other drink. A good example is the legendary Martini of Winston Churchill, who would simply look in the direction of France rather than use Vermouth. Whether an old bulldog like Churchill would have bowed to anyone is a matter of hot debate. While this method, also known as a Naked Martini, is a good way to drink chilled gin neat, it is not really a "cocktail" in the truest sense of the word. A cocktail is a mixture of ingredients. This is not just a purist argument; a good dry vermouth is what helped create the mythos that makes the martini the quintessential American drink.

Best with: Any gin you like the taste of will work well. Navy Strength gins can be a little bracing. Try a few different vermouths and find one that you like the taste of. [1]

> 4 parts gin
> 1 part dry vermouth
> Put ingredients in a glass with ice cubes, stir.[2]
> Strain into a glass and serve straight. Garnish with a lemon peel or green olive.

---

[1] If you want to follow Winston Churchill's recipe, pour the gin in a glass and nod in the direction of France. You may also need a compass. Though we should say , if Winston Churchill was not able to obtain French Vermouth because of World War II, he may have opted to drink his martinis as gin in a glass, which is a pretty good reason for skimping on the Vermouth.
[2] The stir vs. shake debate still rages on with the martini. Shaking will melt slightly more ice in your martini, and some prefer the colder, slightly more dialed back version of the martini. Its not inferior (do not let critical biases interfere with your drinking!), simply different.

Essential Cocktail #5: The Negroni

Elegant, complex and above all, simply easy to remember. The quintessential "equal parts" cocktail, the Negroni marries sweet, herbal, and bitter flavors all together. The Negroni is traditionally an aperitif. The Negroni's origins trace back to Italy, where it was reportedly designed to be a strengthened version of the Americano (which is just Campari, Sweet Vermouth, and Seltzer). For those who have not yet fully adventured into the world of Campari, let this drink be your guide. Campari may be an acquired taste, but for the gin drinker who wants to appreciate all that gin has to offer, Campari is a taste worth acquiring.

The Negroni is a palate-cleansing, quintessential sipping drink. It does not taste as strong as one might one expect for a drink which is equal parts of three different liquors. The flavors are complex, and different gins can highlight or downplay different elements in the cocktail. Take a more floral gin and you start to taste the bright herbal notes in your sweet vermouth. Take a classic styled juniper-forward gin and it highlights the unique bitter orange notes from the Campari. Suffice to say, there are few wrong ways to enjoy a Negroni and few gins that make a bad one.

Best With: Complex herbal gins with a juniper centered approach work well here, like Barr Hill or Southern Gin.

> 1 part gin
> 1 part sweet vermouth
> 1 part Campari
> Stir in a glass with ice, garnish with a sliver of orange rind.

Essential Gin Cocktail #6: The Ramos Gin Fizz

There are a few gin cocktails which, by the addition of egg white, take on a rich frothy character (e.g. Clover Club). Meanwhile, there are a few gin cocktails which add cream to come up with a rich almost dessert-like character (e.g. Alexander). There is one cocktail which marries both cream and egg white: the Ramos Gin Fizz, sometimes called the "Breakfast Cocktail," which looks like a citrus and gin milkshake. It originated in New Orleans in the last nineteenth century, but it has endured to this day despite its onerous preparation routine. One New York City gin bar in 2011 even tried to put this cocktail on tap. When made properly, this cocktail can win friends among gin connoisseurs and ginophobes alike.

Best with: While I find that as a rule all citrus forward gins work well, higher proof gins like a Navy Strength will help the gin hold its own (e.g. Plymouth Navy Strength, Perry's Tot Navy Strength).

3 parts gin
2 parts citrus juice (traditionally half lemon and half lime)
2 parts simple syrup
3 parts heavy cream
1 egg white
2 dashes of orange flower water
Seltzer
The instructions are important on this one.
Shake citrus juice and egg white first for about 15-20 seconds. Then add gin, syrup, cream, orange flower water, and ice to your shaker. Shake again, this time for about 30 seconds. Fill glass halfway with club soda, then strain into glass. When in polite company, the froth on top necessitates a straw.

Essential Gin Cocktail #7: The Corpse Reviver #2

Dating back to The Savoy Cocktail Book, the Corpse Reviver has deservedly undergone a renaissance in the last few years. Once an obscure "fire in your head" (hangover) remedy, the Corpse Reviver is now a staple of top notch bar programs around the world. The perfect balance between sour, bitter, sweet, and savory, the Corpse Reviver is a stunning way to showcase what a gin can do, and is dead easy to remember.

Best With: A strong juniper-forward gin (e.g. BIG Gin, Tanqueray), but I've found that some gins made with a neutral grape spirit base add a really unique floral character that complements the herbal notes from the absinthe (e.g. G'vine Floraison, Seneca Drums Gin).

1 part gin
1 part lemon juice
1 part Cointreau (Triple Sec or any other orange liqueur, Curacao will do in a pinch)
1 part Cocchi Americano
1 dash of absinthe
Combine in a shaker with ice. Shake, strain, and serve straight up.

Chapter Seven

The Gin
& Tonic

THE TALE OF TONIC

The tale of tonic starts with the bark of the cinchona tree, which the indigenous Quechua peoples of South America introduced to Europeans. The cinchona tree quickly gained popularity among Europeans for its anti-malarial properties. Once plantations were founded, the price of quinine fell and it was used to treat fever more widely. By the time of Wellington's Peninsular War against Napoleon in the early nineteenth century, small bottles of quinine bark were carried by many soldiers; this followed lessons learned by an outbreak of malaria in Walcheren during an invasion of the Netherlands, where thousands of soldiers died from the disease. Colonial employees of the British and Dutch Empires were given either the powdered version or a stick extract of it to prevent Malaria in their tropical colonial outposts.

Given the unpalatable bitter taste of the powder, various innovative ways were found to make it easier to take the medicine; this included mixing it with fruit juice, sugar and even gin. Colonial soldiers and officers returned to the UK with a taste for this concoction and, between Erasmus Bond and Jacob Schweppes, the sparkling Tonic Quinine Water that we know today was born.

Whilst popular in the UK by the mid-nineteenth century, the Gin & Tonic did not gain popularity in the United States until after the Second World War. This was due, in part, to a heavy marketing campaign from Canada Dry and Schweppes produced in 1953.

In the twenty-first century, the boom in high-end gins led to the creation of premium tonic waters. The market's evolution continues today with the introduction of tonic syrups and companion tonics.

THE TASTE OF TONIC

Each Gin & Tonic was tasted with 25ml Plymouth Gin and 60ml of tonic water, in an Old Fashioned glass with two large pieces of ice and no garnish.

FEVER-TREE

Widely hailed as the first premium tonic water and an inspiration for scores of others, Fever-Tree was launched in 2005 in the UK, and shortly after around the world, including the United States. Fever-Tree was trying to meet demand for a premium mixer to go with premium gins. It was unusual when introduced, as it uses natural, not synthetic quinine.

Neat: Clean, with citrus and a good bitter-sweet balance. Very fresh, with a long finish.

With Gin: Clean and crisp. The gin shines through and there is no cloying aspect. This works best with bold and complex gins.

PETER SPANTON #1 LONDON TONIC

Peter Spanton Beverages, launched in 2010, offers a range of flavored tonic water including: London Tonic, Cardamom, Mint & Bitters, and Lemongrass.

Neat: Malty, citrus hops and lemon juice on the nose. The tonic has a medium fizz and starts with a strong, earthy bitterness mixed with fresh lemon juice and some malty notes. This has a powerful flavor, bringing something different to the market. The Cardamom variety is spicy and sweet, with a hint of dry apple; the Mint & Bitters provides mint-chocolate-chip flavors, which is rather eccentric but brilliant; and the Lemongrass is zesty, spicy and a great mixer for gin.

With Gin: This mixes quite well with the gin, with the spirit's flavor to start and then the tartness of the citrus and earthy bitterness of the tonic and a touch of dry juniper towards the end.

SCHWEPPES (USA)

The most popular tonic water in the world, Schweppes Indian Tonic Water was first created in the 1870s and is now available worldwide. There are variances in Schweppes tonics around the world, with the UK's being more zesty and less sweet, the EU variety being cleaner and less cloying, and the Japanese Schweppes being balanced, with a bitter-sweet zestiness.

Neat: Bitter and earthy, with citrus reminiscent of citric acid and a very bitter, cloying finish. In a direct comparison to Schweppes UK, it seems to be sweeter, due to the use of high fructose corn syrup. It has an interesting taste that is both very bitter and slightly sweet. Simple, yet serviceable.

With Gin: Anise and licorice come through quite a bit and the finish is quite sweet. A slight cloying aftertaste and not as crisp as its contemporaries.

Q TONIC

Waving the flag for boutique tonic in the USA, Q Tonic was founded in 2007 and is based in Brooklyn, New York. It is sweetened with organic Mexican agave and is made using hand-picked quinine from the Peruvian Andes. Q also make a high-end Ginger Ale, Club Soda and Cola.

Neat: Soft, earthy nose with a hint of lemon and a fizz of small intense bubbles. The flavor is also soft and earthy with citrus and lemongrass. The finish is long, earthy, and bitter with the taste of cinchona bark. The tonic is clean, not too sweet and slightly reminiscent of the taste of tonic syrup.

With Gin: A good combination, with a fine balance between spirit and mixer. The sweetness and character of the gin comes through at the start and middle and the tonic dominates the finish. With a little ice melt the drink comes alive, being refreshing and not too sweet.

1724

A Spanish tonic water, the style of 1724 reflects the Gin Tonicá that is popular in the country. 1724 uses quinine harvested from 1,724 meters above sea level in Peru.

Neat: A light, nose with some sweet citrus. The tonic has small, intense bubbles and is very clean and fresh to taste. There are notes of lime to start, which give way to more citrus and a long, earthy, bitter finish with very little of the cloying nature of some soft drinks, making this very easy to drink on its own.

With Gin: The tonic brings out the citrus and sweetness of the gin, and tends to amplify and complement flavors rather than mask or modify them. Bitterness from the tonic remains on the finish, with a good amount of earthiness. Not cloying.

THOMAS HENRY

A German tonic water named after the apothecary from Manchester, England, who is attributed with the first production of carbonated water in 1773. Thomas Henry also makes an Elderflower Tonic Water, a Tonic Syrup, specially formulated bitters, and cookies that are designed to accompany a Gin & Tonic.

Neat: Clean, crisp, fresh and light, with a good balance of citrus and sweetness. High-to-medium level of fizz and a depth of flavor, with some earthy bitterness and sweet citrus at the end.

With Gin: Excellent; the full flavor of the gin comes through. Clean and crisp, with a brilliant balance and added bitter and fresh characteristics from the tonic. Clean, crisp and refreshing, with brilliant balance; exactly what a Gin & Tonic should be.

EAST IMPERIAL

Made using Japanese, rather than the more typical Peruvian quinine, East Imperial Tonic water is inspired by a recipe from 1903. With a dryer flavor profile than other tonics, it brings new potential to the drink.

Neat: Fascinating, a tonic that throws away the rulebook. The nose has hints of cream, raspberry and blackberry. The fizz is large and explosive in the mouth, but subsides quite quickly to leave flavors of soft vanilla and hints of dry berry. Despite some confectionery-like notes, the tonic itself is very dry, like a fine dark chocolate and the finish is one of pure earthy cinchona bark. So different, but with a lot of potential.

With Gin: Unlike any other tonic out there it brings the sweetness of the Plymouth out and adds a dry creaminess to the mix. There is very little sweetness from the tonic at all. The gin has room to breathe and the citrus and spice come through. An elegant drink with a long, dry, bitter finish.

TONIC SYRUP

Tonic is also sold in syrup form, to which you can add your own carbonated water. The condensed nature of the syrup not only reduces the cost of shipping, but also allows drinkers to experiment with different levels of dilution and other uses in cocktails. Notable brands include: John's Premium, Tomr's Tonic, Jack Rudy and Liber & Co. Many notable cocktail bars such as PX in Alexandria, Virginia and Saxon & Parole in New York City make their own tonic syrups in house and serve with their gin and tonics.

COMPANION TONICS

These are tonic waters designed to specifically complement the botanical notes of a certain gin. 6 O'Clock Tonic in the UK is a good example, as is the Spanish tonic made to complement Broker's Gin.

GARNISHES

The subject of Gin & Tonic garnishes can be a controversial one. Much debate is held over the use of lemon or lime, or both (the latter is known as an "Evans" Gin & Tonic). As always, it is important for the individual drinker to make their own choice.

In Spain, a popular variation on the Gin & Tonic known as a Gin Tonicá is famous for using lots of garnish. The Gin Tonicá is served in a large balloon glass filled with ice and creative garnishes consisting of a various fruits, flowers or herbs that reflect the botanicals in the gin. The balloon glass helps to keep the drink cold, the tonic fizzy and concentrates the aromas of both the gin and garnish. Companies like Infugintonic produce garnish infusion bags that make it easy to add extra flavor to homemade Gin Tonicás without the effort of preparing complicated garnishes.

MAKING A GIN & TONIC

Preferred ratios for mixing a Gin & Tonic vary from 1:1 to up to 6:1 in favor of the tonic water. In many places, a drinker's choice of garnish is just as wide. In fact, the Gin & Tonic is such a personal subject that even the authors of the book couldn't even agree on a single recipe to suggest, so here is one from each of them.

Aaron's Gin & Tonic Recipe

I like to use a beer stein for my Gin & Tonics, but any suitable tall glass will do. My favorite gins for a G&T are Martin Miller's Westbourne Strength or a floral contemporary gin such as Dorothy Parker or Green Hat. I also prefer Fever-Tree or Schweppes Indian Tonic here. I like just a hint of sweetness from my tonic water. This drink maintains a bright lime aroma the entire way through it. For gins which are a little milder, cut the lime half in half.

> 2 parts gin
> Half a lime, juice and peel
> 3 parts tonic water

In a glass add gin, squeeze and drop in half of a rinsed, fresh cut lime. Add tonic water and stir drink once quickly with spoon. Add ice to fill.

David's Gin & Tonic Recipe

> 50ml of gin
> 120ml of tonic water
> No garnish

Take a chilled Old Fashioned Glass. Add 50ml of gin. Add 120ml of tonic water. Add three large piece of ice. No garnish, but allow to mellow for 20 seconds before drinking.

Appendix I:

Further Reading & Useful Links

For updates to this book check out www.craftofgin.com.

For a list of distillers, check out the American Distilling Institute's Directory, online at www.distilling.com/pub.html

GIN REVIEWS

www.theginisin.com

www.summerfruitcup.com

www.unitedstatesofgin.com

TONIC WATER

6 O'Clock Tonic — www.bramleyandgage.co.uk

1724 — www.1724tonic.com

East Imperial — www.eastimperial.net

Fentimans — www.fentimans.com

Fever-Tree — www.fever-tree.com

Markham — www.markham.es

Peter Spanton — www.peterspantonbeverages.com

Q Tonic — www.qdrinks.com

Schweppes UK — www.schweppes.com

Schweppes USA — www.schweppesusa.com

The Original Tonic — www.theoriginaltonic.com

Thomas Henry — www.thomas-henry.com

TONIC SYRUPS

Five by Five Tonics Co. — fivebyfivetonics.com

Jack Rudy — www.jackrudycocktailco.com

John's Premium — johnstonic.weebly.com

Liber & Co — www.liberandcompany.com

Tomr's Tonic — www.tomshandcrafted.com

GARNISHES

Infugintonic — www.infugintonic.com (Gin & Tonic Infusion Bags)

OTHER USEFUL BOOKS

Coates, Geraldine. *The Mixellany Guide to Gin.* New York: Jared Brown, 2012 ISBN: 978-1-907434-28-0

Dillon, Patrick. *Gin: The Much Lamented Death of Madame Geneva, The Eighteenth Century Gin Craze.* Boston: Justin, Charles & Co, 2004. ISBN: 978-1-9321-1225-2

Miller, Anistatia R. and Jared M. Brown. *Shaken Not Stirred: A Celebration of the Martini.* New York: William Morrow, 2013. ISBN: 978-0-06-213026-6

Regan, Gaz. *The Bartender's Gin Compendium.* Bloomington: Xlibris Corporation, 2009. ISBN: 978-1-4415-4688-3

Warner, Jessica. *Craze: Gin and Debauchery in the Age of Reason.* New York: Basic Books, 2002. ISBN: 978-1-5685-8231-3.

Appendix II

Gin Genius Questions

CHAPTER 1 - ON GIN

Q1   What is meant by a Cary Grant Gin?
Q2   What is the ABV of a Navy Strength Gin?
Q3   Who was the Roman Philosopher who saw the potential for fla-
      voring food with juniper berries?
Q4   Who patented a column still in 1822?
Q5   Who was the last big company to make an Old Tom Gin?

CHAPTER 2 - ON MAKING GIN

Q1   What is the advantage of low temperature distilling?
Q2   Which gins use the following spirit bases?
      [a] Honey [b] Sugar beet [c] Whey
Q3   Name two gins that use single botanical distillation and then blend
      the distillates to make their gin?
Q4   What is Bathtub Gin?
Q5   What are the two main methods of distilling gin?

CHAPTER 3 - JUNIPER & OTHER BOTANICALS

Q1   Approximately how many species (including sub-species) of juniper are there?

Q2   What flavors do coriander and cilantro typically add to gin?

Q3   What are the three types of iris that are used to make orris root?

Q4   What are the six most popular botanicals to be used in gin?

Q5   What botanicals work particularly well with cinnamon?

CHAPTER 4 - ON TASTING GIN

Q1   What variety of Juniper does Cascade Mt. use?

Q2   What gin (that we reviewed) has the highest ABV?

Q3   What is the name of a gin from Mississippi?

Q4   How many gins (that we reviewed) state they use cucumber as a botanical?

Q5   Who makes Dorothy Parker Gin?

CHAPTER 5 - MEETING THE MAKERS

Q1   Which distiller is rather partial to strawberry milkshakes?

Q2   What was the inspiration behind the style of Bluecoat Gin?

Q3   How many types of coriander does Dr. J Gin use?

Q4   Which distiller makes both Aged and Navy Gins?

Q5   What are the alternative professions for each distiller?

CHAPTER 6 - GIN COCKTAIL CANON

Q1   What ingredient and key component of the Aviation was out of production for most of the 20th century?

Q2   Should a Martini be "shaken" or "stirred"?

Q3   Name an "equal parts" cocktail from the gin canon i.e. any cocktail which includes x ingredients in the same amounts.

Q4   A Tom Collins made by substituting simple syrup for honey is known as what?

Q5   Which onerous cocktail requires orange flower water?

CHAPTER 7 - GIN & TONIC

Q1   In what year was Q Tonic founded?

Q2   What is name of the lemon/lime combination garnish for a Gin & Tonic?

Q3   How do you make a Spanish Gin Tonicá?

Q4   What is a "companion tonic"?

Q5   What is the name of the tree that natural quinine comes from?

Answers on page 76

ANSWERS

CHAPTER I - ON GIN

A1   A nickname for a gin in the Trans-Atlantic style: a mix in flavor of the Classic British and the Contemporary American.

A2   57% ABV.

A3   Pliny the Elder.

A4   Anthony Perrier.

A5   Gordon's, who discontinued their variety in the 1960s. Hayman's released their Old Tom Gin in 2007; Goldencock Gin from Norway has been produced continuously since the 1950s.

CHAPTER 2 - ON MAKING GIN

A1   Flavors are better preserved and gentle flavors are less "cooked." This is illustrated well by orange peel, which becomes more of a marmalade flavor when overheated.

A2   [a] Comb9; [b] Dr. J; [c] Knockeen Hills Heather.

A3   Gin Mare, Leopold's, Moore's, Sloane's, Sacred.

A4   Although the term dates from Prohibition, today it is a nickname for cold-compounded gin; gin made by infusing botanicals or using essences rather than distillation; Master of Malt make a gin by this method known as Professor Cornelius Ampleforth's Bathtub Gin.

A5   [1] Botanicals are added directly to the pot still, producing bolder flavors. It may be difficult to get the balance right, and is less suitable for botanicals with lighter flavors. [2] Gin Basket Method— This is better when working with more delicate flavors, like those of flowers.

CHAPTER 3 - JUNIPER & OTHER BOTANICALS

A1   Around 70 including species and subspecies.

A2   Coriander: citrus and herbal notes. Cilantro: sharp, leafy, herbal, and slightly soapy citrus flavor.

A3   Iris Germanile, Iris Palida, Iris Florentina.

A4   Juniper, coriander, angelica, lemon, orange and orris root.

A5   Cardamom, orange, nutmeg.

CHAPTER 4 - ON TASTING GIN

A1   Juniperus Occidentalis

A2   Watershed Gin (50.0%ABV)

A3   Bristow (Cat-Head Distillery)

A4   Three

A5 New York Distilling

CHAPTER 5 - MEETING THE MAKERS

A1 Sion Edwards

A2 Observation of drinkers squeezing lemon or lime into their drink before even tasting it - they desire more citrus.

A3 Five.

A4 Paul Hletko (FEW Spirits)

A5 Robert Cassell—Farmer (though trained in nuclear medicine); Paul Hletko—Something creative; John Walters—Perfumist; Tom Warner—Professional Rugby Player; Sion Edwards—Electrical Engineer

CHAPTER 6 - GIN COCKTAIL CANON

A1 Creme De Violette

A2 Trick question: it's whatever you prefer. There is no right way to make a Martini.

A3 Negroni or Corpse Reviver #2

A4 The Bees Knees

A5 The Ramos Gin Fizz (half credit for "Breakfast Cocktail").

CHAPTER 7 - GIN & TONIC

A1 2007

A2 "Evans-style"

A3 Take large balloon or coupe glass, fill with ice, add a double measure of gin and then your tonic. Garnish with peels, fruits or flowers—sip and savor.

A4 A tonic water designed exclusively to complement that character of specific gin.

A5 Cinchona Tree (*Cinchona Officinalis*)

INDEX

CPSIA information can be obtained at www.ICGtesting.com
Printed in the USA
LVOW06*0052130315

430367LV00002B/5/P